DETENTIuN

CAUTIONARY TALES FROM THE WORLD OF EDUCATION

by
Oliver Gray

Sarsen Press

Published by Sarsen Press

Copyright: Oliver Gray, 2021

Cover design and layout by Richard Williams

Contact Oliver Gray at www.olivergray.com

ISBN: 978-1-5272-9804-0

Printed and bound by CPI Group (UK) Ltd, Croydon, CR0 4YY

ACKNOWLEDGEMENTS

Inspired by Annabel and Lucy, who are now both working in education.

Dedicated to the memory of inspirational educators who are no longer with us: Richard Shephard, Wolf Lingstädt, Hans Brinkmann, Bill Hubert and Roy Bone.

Written for Birgit Gray.

ASSEMBLY

ASSEMBLY

The other day, my little four-year old granddaughter Ella received her report from her pre-school. It ran to two full, closely-typed pages, going into great detail about her character and everything she had learnt. I reflected on how that contrasted with the reporting system in Germany, which consists of a number from 1 to 6, with no further comment.

Can any value judgements be made, or conclusions drawn, from these two very different approaches? German students, after all, have much higher levels of attainment than their UK counterparts, despite the fact that they start school a full two years later. I thought about Ella's mother, my daughter Annabel, who, after ten years in primary teaching, now has a business whose *raison d'être* is to educate parents about what their children are learning, and how they learn it. Current practice in primary mathematics, and, in particular, the phonic approach to learning to read are so different from what the parents did at school, that many of them feel baffled and intimidated. Then I considered my other daughter. Lucy works for a charity that supports schools that are twinned with farms and grow all the food for their own school lunches. Such innovations are quite inspiring, and thankfully bear no resemblance to the kind of regimented existence I had to tolerate in my own school days. I'm one of those many people who went straight from school to university, and then straight back into school as a teacher, so my entire life has been tangled up in the education system. I've experienced the class-ridden and very unequal nature of British education, and also the far more egalitarian systems that dominate in Germany and France. As a teacher, I've had to cope with never-ending see-saw changes that have rarely resulted in improved learning or outcomes. A good example of this was "grammar is compulsory", followed by "grammar is absolutely forbidden", followed by "grammar is compulsory again", all within a couple of decades.

Education is something all of us have in common, but it's a strange old beast. I thought that writing down some of my experiences over the years might be both therapeutic and possibly interesting for potential readers. I hope it is.

Chapter 1
SCHOOL DAZE

(i.) Primary Colours

Surprisingly, my destiny to be a socialist was defined by the fact that I went to a private school. My parents had very little money and did that peculiarly English thing of denying themselves almost everything in order to give me a private education. What they didn't know, and never realised, was that it was an awful institution and that I would have got a much better education at one of the local state schools. At least I wasn't a boarder, and could come home every evening.

I've often wondered what my parents' motivation could have been? I fear it was that they didn't want me interacting with the "lower classes", which was farcical, because my family was barely middle class. The thing was, as I have found when delving into family history in recent years, that the Grays used to be wealthy and successful, but somehow we ended up as the branch of the family that missed out. However, poor Father still had to interact with family branches such as the Olivers and the Wimberleys, most of whom still had great wealth, based on a colonial past in the coffee trade from India. Of course, they sent all their children to private schools and somehow, I don't think Father could cope with the shame of not keeping up with them. But it meant that we were permanently short of money and never went on holidays or out for meals.

My elder (but not eldest) sister was responsible for my early education. She was nine years older than me (the other one was twelve years older). I was a classic post-war "afterthought", preceded by a stillbirth spoken of in hushed tones as "Little Willie". I therefore grew up pretty much as an only child, but my sister, a born teacher, taught me to read at home. I can clearly remember her voice as she taught me to spell the word "beautiful" by singing the letters out loud in a rhythmic way. My greatest spelling achievement was a label attached to an old chocolate box my mother gave me to keep precious things in. The label read: "Privet. Trespasers will be prosecutecuted".

Both my sisters went to the local Rudolph Steiner school, which was also private, but a lot cheaper. I don't think my parents realised the extent to which that place was rather like a cult, with very odd practices and religion-based conventions. I was sent there for one year at the age of five, but I can remember nothing except, one day, having to trot around in a horse's head at a school fête. Some of the conventions practised there included "eurythmics", a kind of keep-fit dance that entailed throwing wooden rods round a room. Children weren't supposed to have their hair cut until they had lost all their milk teeth – something that I thought was quite cool in the hippie era. Mick Fleetwood attended this school and retained the long hair habit for a lifetime.

Steiner schools, also known as Waldorf schools, are to be found world-wide and are based on the teachings of Rudolf Steiner, an Austrian academic and philosopher who wrote vast tracts of teachings. On the face of it, his ideas for education sound attractive, as set out in the official Steiner creed. Education, it says, should:

- *work for all children, irrespective of academic ability, class, ethnicity or religion*
- *take account of the needs of the whole child – academic, physical, emotional and spiritual*
- *be based on an understanding of the relevance of the different phases of child development*
- *develop a love of learning and an enthusiasm for school*
- *see artistic activity and the development of the imagination as integral to learning*

All fine, but on the down side, there is plenty of controversy to be found in Steiner's teachings.

His credo of "Anthroposophy" forms the fundamental principle of Waldorf education, which bizarrely is based on a belief in reincarnation. The Waldorf curriculum's emphasis on a late start to learning is determined by the pace at which souls "incarnate". So, for example, Steiner believed that illnesses in our current lives can be explained by health problems in previous ones. This leads on to a belief that vaccination against diseases is irrelevant, because their roots lie in a different life. However, despite Anthroposophy being the basis of the educational philosophy, the beliefs are not intended to be imposed on pupils, and the schools say that parents can choose on behalf of their children on matters such as vaccination.

More worrying still was a strong element of racism in Steiner's beliefs. He considered that black people were marked by "instinctual" life, as opposed to the "intellectual" life led by Caucasians. He also believed that each race had a geographical location where they should live, and that therefore black people in Europe were inappropriate. These opinions appear in his lectures rather than his educational writings, and fly completely in the face of Steiner's number one educational rule of embracing "all children, irrespective of academic ability, class, ethnicity or religion". As far as I can see, his beliefs on racial matters were compatible with Nazism.

My perception that Waldorf education is akin to a cult (a perception that has developed in adulthood, since running around in a horse's head at the age of five, I was unable to form much in the way of opinions) was borne out by my eldest sister Faith, who became dedicated to the Steiner cause, espousing a bizarre range of beliefs and dedicating her entire adult life to furthering Steiner's educational philosophy, including refusing vaccinations and, indeed, any medical interventions that weren't herbal.

It was extraordinary that my deeply conservative father was sufficiently enthused by this form of education that he was willing to pay (not very high) fees for both my sisters to stay at the Steiner school right through to A-levels. Equally extraordinary was the policy the school had that academic achievement was secondary to spiritual fulfilment. Thus, neither of my sisters, despite both being very intelligent, got more than two A-levels, and therefore didn't go to university.

One went to a Froebel teacher training establishment and the other studied speech therapy. Considering how keen my father was for me to go to Oxbridge, I can only assume that, for him, it was less important for females to take an academic path.

Thus it was that I was removed from the Steiner school after one year and sent, hair suitably shorn, to the local cathedral school. I'd better not name it, because it still exists (in an apparently much improved and now co-educational form) and I'm probably going to tell you a lot of pretty negative things about it.

Initially there was something called a Junior School, which I guess was the equivalent of a prep school. I remember an extremely daunting headmistress, with whom we had little to do other than be scared when she entered the classroom, and a very warm and kind class teacher called Miss Lowry, who I believe must have taught us all the basics of the three Rs very efficiently.

(ii.) Senior Service

Things only started to go wrong when the time came to go up to the Senior School. It was attached to the cathedral and was housed in old ecclesiastical buildings, I think maybe the Bishop's Palace, so everything was rather grey, dark and intimidating. About a quarter of the boys were boarders, and they were housed in stark dormitories in various buildings along the street that led into the city centre.

I got to school by taking the 56 bus from Edge, the village

where I grew up. My father and I had so little in common that we didn't talk to each other, even though we caught the same bus every morning at 8:10. He stuck his head into either a newspaper or a learned tome of some kind and I would sometimes go so far as to hide behind a hedge until the bus arrived, so I wouldn't have to stand next to him. It's important to understand that he was not intimidating in any way and never threatening towards me at all, but we just didn't have anything to say to each other. Like most parents of that generation, he didn't talk about his rôle in the war and it wasn't until many years later that I discovered that he'd been quite a hero, and heavily decorated for his service.

It was a double-decker bus, so I would go upstairs, where, of course, everyone was smoking. They had those little brass stubbers on the back of each seat, and I do remember stubbing my surreptitious cigarettes while embers cascaded down onto my trousers, causing small burn marks to appear. The bus would pull into the city bus station, from where it was about a ten-minute walk to school, past a huge department store called Bon Marché and, more frighteningly, past the Regal cinema, which would display posters for whatever film was on that week. I have an extremely strong memory of seeing a poster for a film called The Mummy and being so terrified that I couldn't sleep for weeks.

On the corner of Pitt Street was a half-timbered fish and chip shop which had loudspeakers outside, through which were pumped tape recordings of the Light Programme's "Sing Something Simple", with the Mike Sammes Singers. Regardless of whether the chippy was open or not, this music would waft out to entertain the passers-by from morning till night. During most of the time I would walk this route, there was demolition work associated with slum clearance going on. This was, after all, the world of Fred West and, happily, all that housing has now long since been replaced.

On the way to school, I would always meet a street cleaner called Sam. This gentleman clearly had severe learning difficulties, but operated his broom and trolley with aplomb. Actually, maybe his name wasn't Sam, but we assumed it was, because he called everyone Sam. It was a bizarre scene as he called out "Hello Sam" to everyone who walked by, including the women. Everyone replied "Hello Sam" to him too. But my father and, indeed, school staff tried to forbid me to talk to him. This seemed unfair and illogical to me – why shouldn't we greet this harmless chap?

When the time came for me to enter Senior School, discussions took place about whether I should do a "Double Remove". This was a strange procedure, which to this day I don't really understand. There was a class called Remove, which was the bottom class of the secondary part of the school. For some reason, it was possible for certain pupils to skip Remove and go straight into the next class. Apparently, I was the only person in that year who merited this jump and the truth of the matter, I now realize, was that actually I didn't merit it. I think my father saw it as a great compliment and proudly agreed that it would be a good idea, but it was the beginning of what was to turn into a royally cocked-up secondary education. I found myself in a class of boys who were all a year older than me, and I never really caught up.

From being consistently Top Of The Class in the primary section, I now found myself in the lower third of the rankings, where I was to remain until I left. Luckily, my performance in English and languages was enough to cancel out the poor results in mathematics and any form of science.

(iii.) Leave them kids alone

The teachers were a very motley collection indeed. As they were virtually all Oxbridge graduates, they swished around in dark-coloured academic gowns, which made them appear like demented vampire bats. There were some extremely odd characters among them; in fact, none of them at all were what you might call normal. Even though I am sure they're all long since dead, I'm going to change all their names for the purposes of this memoir. They probably have children and grandchildren who are delightfully conventional.

My maths teacher, Mr Marley, was also my Head of House. The school was divided into four Houses, all named after historical bishops. My House was called Wheeler. It was presumably done in order to simplify organisational arrangements, but part of the ethos was to engender a sense of competition between the various Houses. I genuinely believe I must have been born with no sense of competition in my blood, because I could never see the point of this, nor any reason why I was expected to look down on people who happened to be in a different House. Having absolutely no sporting talent or interest, I had little to contribute to this rivalry, but Mr Marley was bursting with pride when I would occasionally have some bland essay published in the school magazine and be credited as a member of Wheeler House.

In an attempt to please, I twice created models made of balsa wood. One was of a church and another was an attempt at Shakespeare's Globe Theatre. By some kind of miracle, these received merit stickers in the school's annual Hobby Exhibition, which once again pleased Mr Marley. Apart from that, he struggled with me because, the harder I tried at maths, the worse I got. My reports always implied that I wasn't trying, which was far from the truth. I was pretty scared of Mr Marley, whose other obsession was checking that our hair wasn't getting too long. In a final and unsuccessful attempt to get into his good books, I briefly joined his after-school Photography Club. This entailed taking black and white shots of various items of still life. However, he tried to insist that my parents should buy me a Pentax camera, which they couldn't afford, so my tenure in the Photography Club was a short one.

Every morning, we all had to file in silence into the cathedral for a twenty-minute Church of England service. This was sufficient to make me a lifelong opponent of organised religion. There was a hymn, a lesson, a series of prayers and finally another hymn, before we shuffled out again at the end, to the tones of the mighty cathedral organ, an element that did influence my later life, as I became a fan of the Hammond. None of the hymns, the psalms, the lessons or the prayers made any sense to me whatsoever, so I didn't believe a word of them.

I still shudder at the thought of those morning services.

When trapped in the middle of a row, I would feel nauseous and generally ill. A few times, I had to run out and be sick. To this day, I am so claustrophobic that I have to sit at the end of a row in the theatre or cinema, otherwise I suffer panic attacks. I also, in my early teens, had recurrent migraines, vicious affairs featuring psychedelic flashing lights, double vision and a searing headache. Illogically, a doctor who my parents consulted diagnosed appendicitis, and my appendix was duly removed. As I had absolutely no symptoms of appendicitis, I have often thought that the surgery was probably unnecessary and that the innocent appendix should still be in place.

Among the many things that baffle me about my father's decision to send me to that school is the fact that he was a lifelong non-believer, in fact quite scornful of Christianity, yet here he was, submitting me to a daily diet of it. Trying to analyse it now, I believe that, as a historian, he liked the idea of me being associated with something that had a long tradition, and he also hoped that all those Oxbridge-educated teachers might turn me into some kind of academic. In actual fact, it was probably the aforementioned snobbishness that was the most important factor, and this was the only private school in the area that was vaguely affordable.

Christianity was a significant part of the education provided at the school, but in a rather odd way. We had several lessons each week of Divinity (now it would be called RE). RE, I think, offers comparative studies of religions, whereas this was simple Bible Study or, put more clearly, indoctrination.

Our divinity teacher was known to us as Holy Joe. His lessons feature particularly strongly in my memory. It surely can't have been that we had more divinity lessons than any others, but that's the way it now seems to me. He was very short and rotund - I think of him as the shape of the Mister Men. He would rest his hands on his stomach as he took it in turns to humiliate us. He gave each pupil the name of somebody from the Bible. I inevitably was Obadiah. Almost everything he taught us was from the Old Testament, and he had a kind of cynical approach to it, whereby he would convey the whole thing as some kind of ludicrous joke, which of course it was.

Despite the fact that he was so jovial and "unholy", he was also prone to terrible mood swings. Without warning, and for no apparent reason, he would suddenly switch from an apparent state of benevolent calm to an uncontrolled red-faced spittle-spurting rage. Propped up next to the blackboard was a cane, and at least once each lesson, one or other of us would be hauled out by the scruff of the neck to the front and battered on the behind with this very painful stick. Upon completion of the punishment, he would switch back to his smarmy smile and continue the lesson as if nothing had happened. Despite being an almost pathetically well-behaved pupil, this happened to me several times.

What would normally occur would be that he would make some joke. This would encourage us to think he was in a good mood, and we would respond in a jocular way. He would then take exception to our smiles and pick one of us, seemingly at random, for the public punishment. Presumably he gained some kind of short-term satisfaction from this, which would, until the next time, restore him to his original state of relative equanimity.

This is a good point to talk about the general concept of corporal punishment. In that school, as in most secondary schools at the time, it was considered completely normal. All the teachers had a cane to hand, and when I look back now, the ones that I respected never touched their sticks and the ones that I hated, feared and scorned were those who wielded them as a matter of habit. You never knew what might offend them and spark them off, so you constantly lived in a state of heightened tension. Sometimes the beating would be administered in front of the class. You had to be careful not to yelp too loudly, as that would qualify you for an extra stroke. On some occasions, you would be hauled out of the classroom into the corridor outside, but the worst times were if you had done something considered really bad and were sent to the headmaster for a full-on beating, known as "six of the best".

The headmaster dealt me a six on several occasions. His technique was to do a run-up across his office, so you could hear his feet approaching, before the frankly agonizing contact of the cane with the quivering buttocks. On a couple of occasions, I showed my wheals to my mother on returning home and could see how upset it made her. It must be awful seeing your offspring being injured, but of course she never said anything to the school, despite sympathising with my sense of injustice. It was simply considered a normal thing to happen, and in my parents' case, of course, they were paying for it. It did contribute to my education in a significant way, however, because it made me resolve never, ever to inflict punishment on another human being, adult or child, and in my entire life I have never hit anybody.

I think my father would have described himself as a disciplinarian, but he didn't physically punish me on any kind of regular basis, which was quite unusual for parents in those days. I remember very clearly the only time he ever formally hit me. I guess I must have been about ten years old and took it into my head to sit on the window sill outside my first-floor bedroom. I think what happened was that he was completely freaked by the thought that I might fall and injure or kill myself, and that sparked off the only response he could think of, which was to take off his slipper, ask me to bend over and thump my bottom with it several times. The scene must have looked hilarious but, as a punishment, it wasn't very effective, because it didn't actually hurt. On the other hand, it did cure me of sitting on window sills, because I was so shocked by his emotional response. Since then, I have spent a lifetime of being ultra risk-averse.

Astonishingly, at school, certain prefects were allowed to cane younger boys. There were two categories of prefect, a House Prefect and a School Prefect. I think the concept behind it was to engender a sense of leadership in certain older pupils, in which case it was a complete failure, because it created a bullies' paradise. Those thugs were given a sense of entitled power, and took great pleasure in wielding it on small, quivering adolescents. As I was a particularly diminutive and wimpy teenager, I was a sitting duck, and developed an intense hatred of those sadistic bastards. If they were in a good mood, they would administer non-physical punishments, and had the power to hand out detentions and lines. Detentions consisted of staying behind after school for half an hour, sitting at a desk and staring straight ahead. You weren't even allowed to get on with your homework or do something sensible or useful with the time. Lines were an even more pointless and time-wasting punishment. To keep myself from dying of boredom from writing a hundred times, "I must not speak during assembly" or "I must always walk on the right in the corridor", I would write a hundred times "I" first, followed by a hundred times "must" etc, which, for some reason, made the task easier.

For me personally, there was an issue, on entering the Sixth Form, that was yet another consequence of the "Double Remove", that had taken place back when I had been eleven years old. Because I remained a year younger than everybody else, I was correctly considered immature and not made into a House Prefect, while everybody else in the class was. By the following year, I had actually turned into a bit of a bolshy rebel, and was considered so anti-authoritarian that I never got made a prefect at all, until the ridiculous extra term that I had to do because the idiotic headmaster fucked up my application to Cambridge. As I now, ironically, was the oldest boy in the school, they were forced to make me a prefect, and I took great pleasure in not issuing a single punishment during that period.

It's worth spending a little time describing some of the rest of the motley crew of teaching staff at the establishment. Most of them had nicknames of some kind. There was a Spud, a Bog, a Plum and various other unlikely titles. Those who didn't have a nickname were simply referred to by their first names: Willy, Jack, Paddy.

For the first few years of my attendance, the headmaster was an outdoors, hiking type. He didn't approve of me, because I was the exact opposite. He taught geography and, for a while, I thought it might be a subject I could excel at. I remember my father being extremely proud when he found me sitting in the garden, aged about ten, drawing unconvincing maps of South America and Africa. The geography lessons at school, however, tended to be more about manganese exports, and the only bits I enjoyed were when you had to work out the heights of hills from contours and calculate distances by moving a piece of string across a map. I remember the headmaster getting absolutely furious with me when, on one occasion, I asked a question about Argentinian beef rearing, to which he didn't know the answer. Rather than just admit this, he shouted at me and told me I was stupid, thus stopping my quest for geographical knowledge in its tracks.

This guy was eventually replaced by another head teacher so terrible that it was scarcely credible that he could ever have been appointed as an educationalist, let alone someone who was supposed to be a rôle-model and figure of respect. His name was Mr Rufus, but we called him Goofus, because his most obvious physical attribute was the most pronounced set of buck-teeth in history. They were virtually horizontal, and because he smoked a pipe, were stained brown as well. Inevitably, he had pungent bad breath and a tendency to be unable to control his spittle, which, if one was unfortunate enough to be sitting in the front row, would encroach across the desk like the incoming tide.

For some reason, he taught us philosophy, of which he seemed to know little. This meant that, at least once a term, he would need to consult Grayngreen, the resident experts on German pronunciation. Roger Green was a pupil who, like me, was doing A-level German, so we were considered to be one entity, known as Grayngreen.

"Um, Gwayngween, the famous German philosopher, how do you pronounce his name again: Is it Immanuel Kant or Immanuel Kunt?"

We would chorus back with great enthusiasm:

"Kunt, Sir!"

Of course, Rufus remained completely unaware of anything untoward:

"Ah, Kunt. Thank you, Gwayngween."

"Yes, Sir. Kunt."

I suppose that, at the time, we weren't conscious of just how poor these teachers were, but I stayed in lifelong contact with a fellow pupil of quite some distinction, who knew all about teachers and teaching. Richard Shephard was an extraordinary character. He came from a poor background but gained a choral scholarship to our cathedral school, while his twin brother attended one of the two local state grammar schools. Richard became a distinguished composer and an eminent headmaster of private schools in Salisbury and York, and if anybody should know what good teaching is, it's him. Until his very sad death in 2020, Richard enjoyed nothing more than reminiscing about the abject uselessness of so many of the staff members.

Let's take them subject by subject. Mr Marley's approach to teaching mathematics was to write complicated calculations and equations in microscopic handwriting on the blackboard and expect us to copy them down and understand them. In tandem with my interest in drawing maps, I did find one branch of maths that I enjoyed, namely geometry, because somehow I could relate to shapes rather than figures. Mr Marley, however, seemed to think that geometry wasn't a worthy field of his subject and avoided it as much as possible.

It's a pity that the printed word doesn't really allow for clear transcription of strange voices. Pretty much all the teachers had some peculiar affectation in the way they spoke. Mr Marley had a strong Cornish accent, and the nearest I can get to articulating his favourite branch of maths is "triggurrr-noom-utree". Because of my "Double Remove", Mr Marley assumed that I was going to be good at everything, including maths, and seemed to take it as a personal affront that I was neither good at it nor remotely interested in it. I can remember a blur of incomprehensible things like sines, cosines and an entire book of "log tables".

Eventually I got demoted to a remedial maths class, presided over, inevitably, by a dodgy cleric of some kind, who was extremely old and doddery. With the help of him and some extra coaching after school, I eventually passed GCE O-level maths, allegedly the first person in my family for several generations to get any sort of mathematical qualification. I still believe it must have been a marking error because, apart from being reasonably able to add and subtract in my head, I remember nothing of the many hours of instruction.

A strong element of any private school in those days was the teaching of classics, in our case, Latin. Latin ended up being quite a strong element in my life, but at the time it caused strife between me and my father. One day I mentioned something some Smart Alec had said to me and I regurgitated, which was a claim that Latin was a "dead language". My father told me that later in life, I would be grateful for having learnt it and indeed, I used it in my adult language-teaching life almost daily. I wouldn't have gained the enjoyment I have from speaking French and German if I hadn't known about declensions and conjugations.

The main reason for my criticism of Latin lessons was the utterly appalling quality of the teaching. The teacher, whom we called Paddy, was also in charge of one of the boarding houses. He would spend most of his time with his back to the class, writing on the blackboard, but he had the unsavoury habit of constantly scratching his bottom. We naturally would stand next to him enthusiastically scratching our own bottoms when going up to the teacher's desk to consult Paddy about the finer points of the declension of "mensa". He, of course, would remain entirely oblivious. He taught us so badly that not one single member of the pretty intelligent class passed O-level Latin. This was devastating for my father. I still have the exam paper, on which I spent the time circling every single word of an extract from Virgil's "Georgix" in pencil, because I didn't understand what I was supposed to do, and needed to ward off the boredom of a ninety-minute exam.

One of the other boarding houses was run by a biology teacher whose nickname was Pugsy. He had a nervous habit of introducing every sentence with the words "basically", "effectively" or "fundamentally", or sometimes all three in succession. He also couldn't pronounce the letter S properly, so we would delight in starting the answer to any of his questions with the word "bashically…" The unfortunate Pugsy was tasked with teaching us about what was called "human reproduction". This was fun for us, because it was common knowledge that he was being cuckolded by a young French teacher called Mr Gibson, but Pugsy did have a couple of children, so presumably understood enough about the mechanics of reproduction to teach us about it.

He put on a short black-and-white film, which contained diagrams of stick people and dolls. I wanted to try and catch him out, so asked him a question that probably enters the mind of any adolescent being taught about sex. I put up my hand and inquired, "Bashically, effectively and fundamentally, shir, when the male ejaculatesh the shpermatozoa into the vagina, why doesh shpermatozoa emerge and not urine?" He did look momentarily confused, but came up with a convincing answer: "Bashically, effectively and fundamentally, a membrane comesh acrossh and sheparatesh the shpermatozoa from the urine." This was most impressive, and Pugsy went up in our estimation.

As they knew my father was a historian, history teachers tended to expect me to be successful in that field. I don't know if it was a natural adverse reaction to parental control, but I never found any interest in history as delivered in that school, because it consisted of learning by heart pages of names of kings and queens, plus the dates of their births, coronations and deaths. History was fact rather than analysis. On the other hand, in a classic example of the way education policy swings in different directions, I was quite shocked when my own children spent so much time on analysis and so little on facts in their history and geography education, that now both of them are left with little understanding of where anything is in the world and how anything in the world came to be. As ever, healthy compromise will probably always be the optimal solution.

One history teacher, Skunk, did teach me one thing that stood me in good stead throughout my own teaching career. If you cut a piece of A4 paper into four quarters, the resulting size is exactly the right shape and size for distributing to the class and asking ten quiz or test questions. These can then be swapped and marked by another pupil, thus cutting down on the amount of marking the teacher has to do. Other than that, history was a dead loss for me.

Another of the history teachers was the Deputy Head. He went by the name of Turkey, because he had allegedly previously lived in that country and liked to talk about it. He taught very badly, and inevitably had a silly voice. In one of a series of incidents caused by my ambitions to be a drummer, I was one day descending a staircase from the Sixth Form Common Room and, as I went, tapped out a drum solo on the banister. Turkey was ascending the same staircase and our paths crossed.

"Hop hat, Hwaay." ("Stop that, Gray.")

"Sorry, Sir," I replied. Of course I wasn't sorry, but I did genuinely mean to tell him that I wished I hadn't done it.

Turkey, however, didn't think I was sorry enough. He thought I was being cheeky.

"Hwaay ... Hi hone hi ha hone a wah!"

("Gray, I don't like that tone of voice.")

Again, not wanting any trouble, I replied in what I thought was a non-confrontational way:

"What tone of voice, Sir?"

"Ha hone a wah, Hwaay. Hee henn hunn!!"

("That tone of voice, Gray. Detention!")

But the detention was well worth it. Within minutes, the rumour spread that my innocent "What tone of voice, Sir?" had actually been "What fucking tone of voice, you fucking prick!" I was a hero.

The second drumming-related incident came courtesy of another Classics teacher, called Bog. Obviously, his actual name was Marsh and we were nothing if not predictable. Bog had a large, bushy, pubic-hair style beard and he also smoked an evil-smelling pipe. To complete the unappetising picture, he also had a pronounced nervous twitch, which would spring into action whenever he got angry, which was quite often.

I had discovered that a particular desk in the Latin room was perfect for drum practice. The song I was working on was "Stay", by the Hollies. I was triumphant when, after mid-morning break and while waiting for the arrival of Bog, I got all the way through the song without a single error. However, when I finished the last finger-thwack, the expected tumultuous applause failed to materialise. Instead there was a deadly silence as I looked up to discover Bog standing over me, hands on hips, in his dark, intimidating Cambridge gown.

Fresh from his break-time pipe, Bog's fury was such that he twitched almost as if he was having a fit. In my terror, I still remember that, as his face convulsed, a light mist of pipe-smoke was emitted from his beard and drifted across the room. He grabbed my arm and whisked me to the Head's office for yet another six very painful strokes of the cane.

I would have done anything to gain revenge for this cruel treatment of a harmless bit of fun. But that would have entailed telling my parents exactly why I had been beaten, and they certainly wouldn't have approved of drumming as a career ambition.

As I write this, it becomes increasingly clear that we pupils were by no means innocent, because we used to take the piss out of the teachers, non-stop. It was relatively harmless, because most of them never realised they were being lampooned. One unfortunate character who only lasted one term was a retired maths teacher whom we called Digger. I think there must have been a teacher shortage or something, because no way should he ever have been in any classroom. There was not a hint of any kind of control as we pupils wandered around the room, threw things and made so much noise that Digger's quaking, croaky voice could scarcely be heard at all. Having largely survived an adult career in teaching, my blood runs cold at the thought of the things we did to that poor chap.

There was a large cupboard in one of the classrooms, used for storing stationery, and one day we fulfilled our ambition to get the entire class of 20 into that cupboard. We did this by going up individually at two-minute intervals and asking if we could be excused to go to the toilet. When Digger said yes, instead of using the classroom door, we opened the door to the cupboard and disappeared into it. Digger ended up teaching to an empty room, but at least I suppose it meant it was quieter than usual.

There was one large, slobby boy called Walton, who walked up as Digger sat at his desk, made an enquiry about a maths problem and, as he stood there, crunched a stink bomb beneath his shoe. Anybody who has encountered a stink bomb will know exactly how evil-smelling these items are. Of course, we all reacted by holding our noses, shouting "pooooh" and making retching noises. Digger, by contrast, appeared not to notice anything was amiss and carried on trying to teach as normal.

Plum was our French teacher. We thought he was mad, because he claimed that he spent the summer holidays writing French grammar books. Little did I realise that, as an adult, I would end up doing exactly the same. He naturally had little understanding for what I was doing when, one day, he entered the classroom prematurely to find me dancing on the teacher's desk, doing my Freddie Garrity impersonation. "You were meant for me, everybody tells me so," I warbled, dancing lightly from one foot to the other.

"Gray," intoned Plum, as he wearily filled out the detention slip, "you are absolutely pathetic."

Plum was, though, the only teacher for whom I developed great respect and affection, probably partly because I was good at French and therefore enjoyed his lessons, which were businesslike and efficient rather than inspirational. I have much to thank Plum for.

This applied less to Willy, who taught me German. He was tiny, and his lessons consisted of word-by-word translations of texts by Goethe and Schiller. He had a penchant for puns, which led to several strange and frightening incidents. The pattern was that Willy would make an excruciating pun, a pupil would reply with another one, everyone would laugh, Willy would pitch in with a riposte and for several minutes, a mass punning session would break out. Suddenly, Willy would decide enough was enough, and would fly into a massive rage, shouting and screaming, before charging out of the room and slamming the door. We would sit in cowed and frightened silence until he returned some time later, completely calm, and the lesson would continue as if nothing had occurred.

Martin Gibson, who took over from Plum as French teacher in the Sixth Form, is, I believe, now a priest. At that time, however, he was a young teacher, physically in his early twenties but mentally still back in Infant School. Nowadays he would be hounded out of teaching for his lack of professionalism, but then it was fine for him to spend entire double lessons lying with his feet on the desk reading the Beano, whilst expecting us to write endless notes on Beaumarchais' *Le Barbier de Séville*.

One day in class, Gibson was reading his comic as usual so, thinking that he couldn't see me, I started practising drumming by miming in mid-air. I was obsessed with beat groups at the time. All went well until I inadvertently allowed one of my fingers to hit the table, thus diverting Gibson from Dennis The Menace and alerting him to my non-Beaumarchais-related activity. He was furious.

"Gray!" he squeaked. "Stop being so childishly juvenile!"

This example of tautology was hilariously ironic, coming from the most "childishly juvenile" person any of us had ever met. Obviously under some stress, he berated me for several minutes in this vein.

Shortly after this, I had a piece of luck which greatly helped my academic career. Charging across Rudge Common on my brand new Dawes bike, I braked at the brink of one of the many craters created by the Cotswold stone quarriers, who had worked there two decades earlier. I knew from experience that it was advisable not to plunge straight over without looking first to see whether any courting couples might be entangled in the relative privacy of the grassy crater. As I peered over the lip, the startled eyes that greeted me were those of Mr Gibson. Beneath his flushed face was another flushed face I recognised, that of the wife of Pugsy, the biology teacher. They were clearly researching the finer details of Human Reproduction. I knew her well, because the previous Christmas I had played the angel in the Nativity play, dressed in her see-through nightdress.

What could I do? They had obviously recognised me and I had equally obviously recognised both of them.

"Hello, Sir," I stuttered, before withdrawing from the scene of the crime, remounting my Dawes and retreating.

In the subsequent lessons, he found it hard to look me in the eye, but when he did, I did my best to make my eyes convey the message that I remembered exactly what I had seen. Sure enough, when my next scruffy and incoherent essay on Beaumarchais was returned, it had gained *"A+, très bien!"* This reward for discretion was extended to all further essays and therefore it came as a surprise when, in the actual A-level exam, I barely scraped a B. But it wasn't a surprise to me, or to Mr Gibson.

Something that was noticeable about many of the staff was a tendency to erratic moods and an inability to control their tempers. It was something unfamiliar to me, because both my parents were entirely even-tempered. When hearing news items about controlling husbands who beat up their wives and then apologize profusely afterwards, in order to get them back, I have often speculated about how it must feel to know that at any moment, one could lose control of one's behaviour. My personal response to feeling angry about something, which I do on many occasions, especially about politics, is to fulminate inwardly, grind teeth, feel stressed but never to lash out, either physically or vocally. In some respects, I guess this is arguably a less healthy response. In a later chapter, I will describe what happened on the only occasion in my teaching life when I completely flew into a rage.

(iv.) The Unmentionables

Anybody thinking about private schools in those days will have at the forefront of their mind the "Four Unmentionables": child abuse, bullying, homosexual activity in the dorms and racism. Taking the last one first, I am pleased and rather surprised to report that there wasn't much of it, probably because the demographic was solidly white middle class. Most of the pupils were offspring of families who had done well for themselves and wanted to give their children an advantage, something which was of course a severe error in this case. I do remember a black kid from Ghana who had ritualistic scar marks on his cheeks and we assumed was the son of some chieftain or high-up politician. I am almost certain that racist remarks would have been made, and I do remember one occasion when, probably severely provoked, he lashed out and hit someone. As a result of this, he only lasted one term and disappeared, never to be seen again.

In our class was a very handsome and super-intelligent son of a Saudi prince. Let's call him Nasser Hussein. I remember looking up to him because he was quietly-spoken and utterly charming. He was popular and very much one of the gang, but I do recall that we took the piss out of his accent. In actual fact, his English was probably better than ours. The voice I remember us imitating was an entirely inappropriate Indian one, which we learnt from characters in "Carry On Up The Khyber". He accepted this with complete equanimity, but looking back on it now, yes, our behaviour was certainly racist.

In my class, there was a black boy whose surname was Dove. He was West Indian, I guess from the Windrush generation. His parents lived in a suburb that lay on my bus route home, and he often invited me for tea. His mother made the most wonderful tomato sandwiches, consisting of just Mother's Pride bread, butter, tomatoes and lashings of pepper. I used to consume piles of these, because they were so extraordinarily delicious.

"Why don't you invite your friend to come round for tea one day?" suggested my mother, so I did, and he travelled to my village on the bus with me. As we walked down the lane towards my house, my mother happened to walk out of the front door. Her face was an absolute picture as she took me aside and hissed,

"Is this really your friend?"

"Yes, he's called Dove."

"He can't come into the house."

"Why can't he come into the house?"

"Because Father will be home soon."

"Yes."

"He won't want to see a boy like that in our house, and he wouldn't want you playing with him either."

"Why not?"

"Can't you see?"

"See what?"

"Well, he's different."

It was only then that the penny dropped that it was a racial issue. Growing up in that age and that environment, I genuinely had not identified that there was a visual difference between black and white people. It was the first time that I had become aware of the concept of prejudice.

"But he's a friend. Can't we come in and have some tea? His mother makes me lovely tomato sandwiches."

It was in vain. Mother insisted that I took Dove up to the main road, only played with him there out of sight of our house, and put him on the bus back to town. This, I think / hope I managed to do without making Dove aware of the reason. Just a short incident like this inadvertently formed a very strong part of my education, because it made me a lifelong, dedicated opponent of any kind of racial prejudice or discrimination.

Bullying was probably rife and I, in theory, should have been right in the firing line. I didn't grow taller until my late teens and I've never had anything resembling muscles. I also had something easy to victimise, namely freckles, yet for some reason I genuinely cannot remember ever being bullied. Often, when reading people's memoirs, you hear that they avoided being bullied by being funny, but I don't believe I was particularly funny, so I have no explanation for why I wasn't victimised.

Bullying certainly did go on, though. My small bunch of friends definitely mercilessly took the piss out of a young guy we called Poodle, because he had curly black hair. He also had flat feet and therefore walked in a strange way. We would walk in a line behind him, imitating his gait. I think Poodle remained oblivious to this and I fear the possibly that there was an element of homophobia to our behaviour, because we would mock his high-pitched voice and his reputation as a mummy's boy. He probably was gay, but gayness as such wasn't something that came up particularly, at least unless you were a boarder, which I wasn't.

There was a vulnerable teenager in my class called Peter Wimborne. He also was freckly, but lanky and skinny and his main problem was that he suffered from the most crippling stammer, particularly under stress. One day in English class, poor Wimborne was desperately trying to get out an answer to a question that an English teacher called Spud had asked him. It was agonizing to listen to the poor lad trying to articulate his response as the evil Spud yelled into his face, "Spit it out, boy, for God's sake". I went home and told my mother about it and, to her credit, she did write a letter to the school about the incident. Nothing ever came of it, of course, but I remember

Spud giving me some slightly hunted looks from then on.

I think it's very likely that sexual activity among the boys was common in the dormitories. As a day boy, it didn't impinge on me, and the only thing in that line that I can think of was an activity called "guddling", which would take place in the changing rooms before or after sports lessons. Certain bigger boys would approach smaller ones, stick their hands down their shorts and jiggle their testicles around. It happened to me just once, and it hurt so much that I yelled out loudly, attracting the attention of a passing teacher. My attacker was duly taken off and spanked and I was never guddled again.

The only other thing I remember of that type was a masturbation session, which I witnessed in the changing cubicle after a swimming lesson. A group of about five boys stood around wanking in a circle. This was an example of me being advantaged by being younger than everybody else. Being not mature enough to have any idea of what was going on (it was prior to Pugsy's Human Reproduction film, which anyway didn't mention such activities) I was delegated to stand by the swing doors, keep my eyes peeled and sound the alert for any passing staff. Regarding activities that went on in the dorms, I wouldn't really have cared, unless there was coertion involved, which I now guess quite probably did occur.

Coming finally to the issue of child abuse, all I can say is that, yes, it certainly happened and was known about. As far as I'm concerned, dirty clergyman spanking little boys with canes definitely qualifies as child abuse, but within the cathedral hierarchy there was also a full-on business going on, with senior clergy paying boys for sex. I clearly remember

30

one savvy individual called Broomfield, who made serious money by offering himself to be bummed by one of the most prominent members of the ecclesiastical staff. He wasn't as high-up as the bishop, but not far below him. Broomfield said that it didn't bother him. Rather than perceiving himself as being coerced, he actually volunteered, and as a result had far more pocket money than any of the rest of us.

Broomfield's fees increased exponentially as he realised and exploited the potential for blackmail. At one stage, I remember, the going rate that Broomfield would boast about was £5 a go, which in those days was serious money. I present this information simply as a factual description of what was going on and was generally known about and acknowledged. It's part of the reason that I have very little respect for Christianity and organised religion in general. The levels of hypocrisy from the saintly characters who would deliver their sanctimonious sermons to us every morning at 9 o'clock was utterly outrageous.

(v.) Food For Thought

School dinners ... I am hesitating to talk about them because they are such a rite of passage for everyone. We all have our tales of horrific British school food. However, I have suffered throughout my adult life with being laughed and snorted at for my extreme pickiness with regard to food, and I am certain that most of this can be traced back to lunch times at school. We would march in a crocodile over to a building that was part of the cathedral complex. Here, in a dark cellar, we would sit at long tables, each presided over by one teacher, and be forced to eat whatever was put in front of us. In this post-war era, waste was considered a crime and not eating something, just because you didn't like it, was not an option.

Everybody I know loves mashed potato, except me. Almost every day, this was the principal vegetable piled onto one's plate by the master who doled out the food at the end of the table, before handing the plate to the first pupil, who passed it along to the second, etc, etc. These mashed potatoes invariably had lumps and black bits in them and even writing about this is making me want to retch. "Consistency" is the element that makes much food unpalatable and the consistency of mashed potatoes has made me phobic of them to this day.

There is no rhyme or reason to taste in food. For example, my favourite school puddings were semolina and tapioca, normally with a spoonful of jam plonked on the top. While all the rest of my colleagues turned their noses up and forced it down under protest, I absolutely adored this sweet sludge, which probably wasn't actually a million miles in consistency from mashed potato.

I remember my mother being extremely proud when I came home and announced one day that I had been crowned Prune Eating Champion of Wheeler House after I consumed thirty-seven prunes at one sitting, lining up the stones all the way around the edge of my plate. This superhuman effort did gain me a lot of kudos from my contemporaries. You would think it would have caused the most appalling stomach upset, but it didn't. My subsequent lifelong inability to eat anything with lumps in it, or tough and fatty meat of any kind, can certainly be put down to being forced to eat it in my youth, but it was indeed part of the post-war culture. Even at home, my father would never let me leave the table until my plate was completely empty.

At the end of the table sat Mr Marley, and if you were lucky (ahem), you would be chosen to sit next to him and engage in conversation. We all lived in dread of this privilege, because it was so forced. As well as his Cornish accent, he had a nervous habit of coughing between every sentence. To be fair, he did put his hand in front of his mouth, but in such a way that pieces of food would still escape and threaten to land on the plate of whoever was sitting next to him. Mr Marley taught me the word "condiment", which to my knowledge I have never used in adult life. I remember clearly the first time he said to me "Gray, booooy, please pass me the condiments".

"I'm sorry, sir?"

"The condiments, boy."

"What are condiments?"

"Don't be ridiculous booooy, condiments are salt and pepper."

I didn't say that it might have been simpler if he had just said salt and pepper.

At break time, there was a room in the bowels of the old Bishop's Palace, which served as a tuck shop. There, we were allowed to spend our pocket money on iced buns, which were delicious, and also, surprisingly, on a range of extremely unhealthy sugary sweets with names like Fruit Salad, Black Jacks and Aniseed Balls, ensuring for us all, no doubt, an adult lifetime of shocking dental problems. It was difficult to suck your way through an aniseed ball or a gobstopper before the next lesson, but sucking sweets in lessons would have been unthinkable and certainly would have led to a thrashing. This led to an accumulation of half-consumed aniseed balls in the fluff of our blazer pockets.

Before we were allowed to purchase any of these sweets, we had to consume the compulsory third of a pint of government-provided milk. This arrived in crates each morning and generally was left out in the sun, surrounded by buzzing flies, until we were made to drink it at eleven o'clock. It was Gold Top milk with a layer of cream on the top and invariably, by the time we got to drink it, it was slightly "off". This has led me to suffer a life-long phobia of drinking milk, particularly warm milk. Even the thought of it induces a vomiting reflex similar to that caused by mashed potato.

Talking of blazer pockets, there was, of course, a strict uniform policy. As well as continually monitoring our hair length to ensure it wasn't touching the ears or approaching the collar (a challenging task in the era of the Beatles), Mr Marley would obsessively check our uniform. The upper body was enclosed in a dark blazer with a school badge on the top pocket. My poor mother, never an efficient seamstress, hated having to unpick the embroidered badge and re-attach it each time I grew out of my blazer.

When one had outgrown the grey flannel shorts that had to be worn, even in winter, in the junior school, trousers were an important area for conflict, with much potential for bending the rules. They had to be "charcoal grey", but not light grey or dark grey. They weren't allowed to be tight or narrow-legged and it was compulsory to have turn-ups. Shoes had to have polished toe-caps and anything resembling boots or pointed toes (both fashionable at the time) were forbidden. We all made it our task to bend all these rules as far as possible, but it was difficult, because all the staff were obliged to check uniform compliance every day. I have often thought what a waste of time that was, and that the time should have been better spent in actually giving us a decent education.

Returning to the other end of the body (I won't even start on the subject of ties for fear of fainting in fury), we come to the subject of caps. There was a specific school cap you had to wear, but the constant point of dispute was HOW you wore it. It was unacceptable to pull it down at the front (for example to keep the sun out of your eyes) and equally intolerable to wear it jauntily tipped back. No, it had to be worn completely level. I genuinely was approached numerous times by Mr Marley to be told that I had been spotted in town not wearing my cap "properly". Apparently, this amounted to "bringing the school into disrepute".

(vi.) Arts And Crafts

Creative subjects were distinguished by their complete lack of any creativity. Take music, for example. No instruments were available for us to try out, and music lessons consisted of rehearsing hymns for the following week's assemblies. I did at least learn quite a lot about crotchets, quavers, treble clefs etc, and these have occasionally helped me to answer the odd question on Only Connect or University Challenge. It was a miracle that I spent the rest of my life being dedicated to music, but it was the kind of music that was deemed by the school authorities simply not to exist. Beat groups were everywhere, but not in this school.

Art was another subject in which I ended up semi-traumatised and completely demotivated. Admittedly, artistic skills didn't run in the Gray family. In the art lessons, we were plonked behind easels and invited to copy various photographs and postcards. I recall no teaching of any kind of art history or appreciation, but I did have a brief feeling of success when attempting to copy a postcard of the River Thames and Tower Bridge at night. I took my half-completed masterpiece home, where I found a pot of sparkling gold paint that was around the house because it had been used for decorating Easter eggs. In an attempt to recreate the shining lights of the buildings along the Thames, I added some of this paint to my creation and was full of pride and expecting much praise and a high grade when I took it in the next day. In front of the class, the art teacher held it up, pronounced it to be in shocking bad taste and that metallic paint was on no account ever to be used in any proper art and, with that, ripped the paper to shreds in front of everybody. I didn't cry in public but I did cry when I got home and told my mother about it. She had been very encouraging and also hoped that I would receive acknowledgement for my creativity.

The most upsetting incident in the creative field came courtesy of the aforementioned English teacher named Spud.

I guess he must have been in his fifties and his lessons were particularly nerve-racking, because of his tendency to burst into wild rages at any moment. The problem was that it was impossible to know what would set him off, so you lived in a permanent state of heightened tension in his lessons. As he shrieked, his face would get redder and redder, spit would fly around and the whole thing would end in a huge coughing fit which would last for several minutes, as he spat phlegm into his handkerchief and examined it, presumably fearful that it might contain blood. As this occurred, all we could do was sit in our seats and shiver in terror.

Personally, I tended not to be scared of Spud, because I was good at English. He loved my essays and always selected them to be included in the end-of-term school magazine. Sometimes he would pick up my exercise book and read out extracts from my homework, as an example to the class of high quality writing. It was therefore rather unexpected when, one day, he took exception to something I'd written. My staple reading matter at the time was magazines called War Picture Library, which invariably featured Stukas and Spitfires plunging from the sky and exploding in smoke. The verb often used to describe the smoke was "belching", as in "smoke belched from the stricken aircraft". I had no reason to think there was anything wrong with this word, and so included it in an essay I wrote about an erupting volcano.

The combination of reading trashy war mags and using a word that might have been considered vulgar set Spud off, and I was subjected to the full explosion in my face. As I cowered in my seat, head lowered and shaking in fear, the onslaught predictably ended in one of his traditional coughing extravaganzas. The whole thing lasted for quite some time, before he ended up behind his desk, head in his hands and a phlegm-filled hanky at his side. Once again, I told my mother about this and, as usual, she sympathised but didn't do anything about it.

I thought I'd got my revenge on Spud when later joining his after-school "Literary Society". As I was considered the school expert on all things German, I penned a largely-plagiarised critique of Goethe's Faust and read it out to the uncomprehending group, complete with quotes in German. Spud was severely intimidated by being confronted by someone who knew more about a subject than he did, and promptly nominated me for an end-of-term award, which was presented to me by the mayor in the Regal Cinema. Things ended happily for Spud, who we assumed was not only a confirmed, crusty old bachelor but also was bound to die young of consumption or something like that. In fact, in late middle age, he suddenly got married and his health improved dramatically.

The remaining artistic endeavour with which I involved myself at school was dramatic productions. "Drama" as such didn't exist as a school subject but there was a local lady who put on the school production each year, for which one had to audition. I applied for a part in Shakespeare's "The Taming Of The Shrew" and was allocated the role of Gremio, I think purely on the fact that I had a similar name. The part was tiny, but was quite a good cameo because I had to shuffle on with a walking stick and a beard that had been applied with glue, make a couple of doddery old-man jokes that got great laughs, and go off again. For the rest of the time I was involved in organising props and backstage preparations.

I should have realised straight away that acting in public was an entirely unsuitable activity for my nervous temperament, because I suffered from appalling stage fright, shaking, shivering, sweating and being convinced I would forget all my words and either faint or shout out something inappropriate in a Tourettes fashion. None of this occurred, of course, and before I realised what was happening, I found myself cast the following year in the lead rôle of George Bernard Shaw's "Androcles And The Lion". In actual fact, the rôles that got all the laughs were the lion itself, plus Julius Caesar, played in gloriously camp fashion by Richard Shephard. Playing Androcles entailed learning enormous numbers of lines. I was utterly terrified and in a state of advanced panic throughout, especially as, by now, I had someone in the audience to impress.

In "The Taming Of The Shrew", another boy called Thwaite had been playing the role of Kate. As it was an all-boys' school, the female parts had to be played by males. This guy had caused much jealousy by going out with one of the most beautiful girls in the local girls' private school, which for some reason was twinned with ours. I have never understood why, but when she turned up to watch the play, she was much more taken with my portrayal of Gremio than the trans role of her boyfriend. I ended up going out with her for more than a year and being utterly hated by Thwaite. He looked daggers at me every day and got his friends to make threats, but as he was even more of a wimp than me, no physical revenge was ever taken.

(vii.) Sporting Life

Sport always features prominently on any private school agenda and this place was no exception. Being small and weedy, sport was something I generally dreaded, although I do remember enjoying the indoor PT sessions. Inevitably, the PT teacher was ex-army and was the only person on the staff who had a Northern accent. Of course this meant that we imitated his voice and, as his name was Stan, we called him "Starn The Marn". Maybe the reason I enjoyed PT was that, in general, there was little in the way of competition and so, whatever you were doing, you did on your own. I used to love climbing up and down ropes. When you reached the ceiling and were able to touch it, it was a great feeling of achievement. Less great were the burn marks on your thighs and palms as you slid back down the rough surface. You had specifically been told not to do this, but by that time your arms were normally so tired that there was no choice.

Other fun things to do in the gym included the three "ups" - press-ups, sit-ups and pull-ups - as well as being knocked over by extremely heavy medicine balls and risking life and limb by attempting to fly over the pommel horse. Sometimes, all of these were combined into exhausting, so-called circuit training. I enjoyed all of these activities, especially during the winter when it was preferable to being outside in the freezing cold, doing something that normally entailed mud.

In the summer, athletics were held outside. Sprinting was something that appealed to me but somehow, no matter how fast I ran, everybody else was faster. A couple of guys in my year, who were county standard athletes, could reach the end of the hundred-yard track before I was even out of the blocks. Trying to do your best and still coming last was a discouraging scenario, but at least I understood the concept of running a race. You just had to get from A to B, and there weren't any strange and convoluted rules you had to learn.

The strangest and most incomprehensible rules belonged to rugby, a game of which I had zero understanding. For a start, considering that the aim was to get a ball over a line at the end of the field, when you wanted to pass to somebody, you had to do so in a backward direction. This was a ludicrous concept that I never comprehended, and there was a strange ritual where you had to stand in a line while somebody threw the ball from the side. I always volunteered to do the throwing because in the line, as you leapt to try to catch the ball, you were very likely to be knocked over and hurt.

Most horrific of all was the simple fact that, if you picked up the ball, several huge people would immediately descend on you and kick shit out of you. At other times, they would grab you round the waist and hurl you onto the ground. As clearly this was not something I wanted to happen to me, I would do my best to make sure that, if the ball was anywhere near me, I ran in the opposite direction so I wouldn't have to touch it. If the ball ever did get into my hands, I simply dropped it on the floor and sprinted away from it. For some reason, this made my fellow players and the sports teachers quite angry, but it made perfect sense to me. During this process, you got freezing cold and covered from head to foot in disgusting mud. How anybody could think that this was sensible or productive way of spending time was, and remains, beyond me.

Cricket was a similar scenario, but for a different reason. I actually understood the rules of cricket, but one of the main problems about the game is that the ball is rock hard and if it hits you, it hurts like hell. I would therefore volunteer for an obscure fielding position called Long Stop. This was at the far end of the field, on the boundary behind the batsman. This was quite nice, because at the border of the field was the railway line from Gloucester to Cardiff, where brand-new diesel trains had just been introduced. Watching them trundle by was a very pleasant diversion. The only way the ball could get to you in this position would be if it had been bowled extremely fast and had been both missed by the batsman, and not caught by the wicket keeper. The trouble was that you then had to throw it all the way from the boundary to the middle of the pitch. This was beyond the capability of my arm muscles and the ball would trickle to a halt halfway there. All around the field, eyes rolled and groans of "For God's sake Gray, you're totally useless" would ring out.

There was one term in which I signed up to play hockey. Luckily or unluckily, I got hit on the head with a hockey stick during the first afternoon, which gave me concussion and excused me from joining in for the rest of the term. The person who had hit me was sent off for raising his hockey stick above the shoulder, apparently forbidden in the rules.

I did a little better when I opted to try out rowing, but not for reasons of sporting prowess. Because I was so small, I was appointed as Cox. This was a job which went entirely against my temperament, because part of it entailed shouting instructions in a loud and aggressive manner. We'd go out on the Sharpness canal and I would yell at the rowers to "give it five", or some such bizarre instruction, then spend the rest of the week nursing a sore throat. We did actually once win a race at a regatta, which meant we were presented with medals by Lord Montgomery of Alamein. I felt quite proud, although all I'd contributed was to manage to steer in a straight line and shout a lot.

I did, surprisingly, have one sporting triumph. During the winter, we were required to do cross-country running. This entailed driving in the school bus out to some woodland in the countryside, and running a course of about five miles. As this wasn't a very appealing prospect, I hooked up with a group of "naughty boys" who told me they had a plan to make things easier. This comprised taking a dramatic shortcut about a quarter of the way round that cut off about three miles. If you timed it right, you could sit in the woods, have a cigarette, some sweets and a natter and then rejoin the runners as they reappeared about a mile before the end of the course.

On the first occasion we did this, I joined in a bit too early and ran the last mile as fast as I could, which meant that I appeared to do extremely well. This absolutely thrilled Mr Marley, who promptly nominated me to be a member of the Wheeler House cross-country team in the forthcoming inter-House competition. Mr Marley was, of course, to be bitterly disappointed, because, during the actual race, there were marshals on the course, who made sure that the shortcut was not an option. I trailed in a distant last and was never again asked to represent the House in any sporting activity. As an adult, I became an enthusiastic runner, enjoying many miles of slowish jogs, which were very good for both physical and mental health and didn't entail competing with anybody.

(viii.) Friends And Neighbours

How do you get to know girls when you are in a boys' school? Well, the aforementioned twinned establishment offered the chance, but only if you were willing to join Plum in his after-school Square Dancing Club. The more macho boys would pretend to be interested in this odd activity, and would wink suggestively at the enjoyment caused by coming into contact with females, but as usual, being a year younger than everyone else, I found this too intimidating. There were, however, girls on the 56 bus home, and it was inevitable that some interaction with them would take place sooner or later. They came from the local secondary modern school and the local Catholic school for girls. In theory, we weren't supposed to mix with them but in practice, this was impossible for anyone to police.

I was already on my predestined path to socialism and incapable of understanding why we were supposed to look down on these people. I found them all delightful and easy to get on with. One good technique was to catch the bus home at the normal time but to get off with the girls at their council estate en route, catch the next bus an hour later, and pretend to my parents that I had been doing an after-school club. I had relationships with several different girls in this way. We called it "going out" but we didn't really go out anywhere, just stood around and chatted.

The same applied to the boys from the local state schools. Because Richard Shephard's twin brother went to one of the grammar schools in town, we would meet up with him and his friends. I generally found I got on with them much better than with my private school colleagues. It was also clear that the education they were receiving was at least as good as ours, and probably better, because it wasn't based on being cut off from the rest of society, as ours was.

At school, I can't say that I had particular friends. I just seemed to rub along pretty much with anybody, but in the village where I grew up, I had two close pals. One was Roger, who went to my school and whose wheeling-dealing, property-speculating father was wealthy enough to have an Aston Martin, in which he drove us into town, in extremely cramped conditions, most mornings. The other boy in our trio was Robert, and he attended a local secondary modern school in Stroud. My parents disapproved of Robert because his family had moved down from the Midlands and had strong Brummie accents. Personally I found this charming, and was completely baffled as to why one should ever evaluate people on either their background, their accent or their schooling. Robert went to a local secondary modern school, which I visited a few times. It was co-educational, very progressive, and seemed to be offering a high standard of education. I felt that I would have been far more at home there.

I started going out with a girl from the village called Rosamund. I would see her in the mornings at the bus stop, heading the opposite way, into Stroud, where she attended Stroud High School, the local girls' grammar school. She had previously been going out with her next-door neighbour, who went to the equivalent state boys' grammar school in Stroud, called The Marling. My pal Roger and I were in the table-tennis team at the village youth club, where we would hang out once a week. I always got on better with the local village lads than with the largely posh people at my school, and, in the main, we weren't frowned upon for being at a private school. At one stage, however, the guy who had been going out with Rosamund decided he wanted to take revenge on me for taking his place. He was too much of a coward to do it himself, so he engaged the local hard nut, a ginger-haired yob called Eric, to do the job for him.

In something that must have resembled a scene from a wild west movie, Eric turned up outside my house one evening and challenged me to a fight. I made sure to stay behind the threshold of the garden gate, so that he couldn't get close to me without trespassing. I failed to see the logic of what he was asking me to do. "But I like you," I said. "I don't want to fight with you". Besides, as far as I was concerned, fighting was associated with potentially getting hurt, so I certainly didn't want to be involved in anything like that. Undeterred, Eric, who turned up with a sidekick, started emptying his pockets: "Chewing gum ... keys ... hanky ... cigarettes," he chanted, as he unloaded the various objects into his mate's hands, before formally raising his fists and squaring up to me. It was all very theatrical, but in vain, as I refused to co-operate. Eventually, as dusk fell, all the items were returned to his pocket and they went home disappointed. Not long afterwards, Eric's mum invited me round to tea. We got on great and became quite good friends.

(ix.) Deutschland 1965

It was when I went on an exchange visit to Germany at the age of 17 that I began to become more interested in education and schools in general, and to realise that there was indeed another way. I ended up spending a month in the small town of Schöningen, near the border with East Germany. These were very happy and intense days for someone with so little understanding of the world.

The school was the "Gymnasium Anna-Sophianeum". *"Gymnasium"*, contrary to appearances, is the German word for Grammar School. The number of private schools in Germany was so small as to be negligible, the entire education system being built on all schools being of equal quality. Germans shook their heads in bafflement at the extraordinary differences between schools in the UK. Nowadays exacerbated even more by the academy system, the concept of people moving house in order to get their children into a better school seemed ludicrous to them.

This isn't to say that the German system was non-selective. There were different types of school; for example, grammar schools functioned alongside vocational schools. Children who were not so academic would more than likely end up in a secondary or vocational school, but there were no value judgements attached to whether your child went to one or the other type of establishment. Selection was mainly based on where your aptitudes lay.

The most obvious and gratifying difference for me as I pitched up in the *"Gymnasium"* was the fact that it was co-educational; yes, there were girls around. Those few weeks were sufficient to transform my shyness into much more natural interaction with anybody I came into contact with. My exchange partner was a boy called Johann and, from the very first day of visiting his class, I was welcomed with incredible warmth by everyone in the school, possibly enhanced by the slight exoticism of my coming from England. All the nonsense that surrounded my schooling at home was delightfully absent. There were no stupid pointless rules, no uniform, nobody commenting on the length of your hair and very little in the way of discipline. This was because the children were all well-behaved and didn't need to be disciplined, herded around and made to conform to silly conventions. Johann, naturally, was horrified and amazed when he came to England and had to attend my over-disciplined, single-sex establishment.

Lessons took place only in the mornings and there were no so-called extra-curricular activities, apart from a small amount of sport. The teaching was very formal and the staff, in stark contrast to my previous experience, seemed uniformly sane, human and willing to interact in a natural way with their pupils. There were no school dinners, as each pupil brought sandwiches, typically *"Leberwurst"* on black bread. There was the same post-war supply of free milk, but luckily there was an option of *"Kakao"*. This was cold cocoa-flavoured milk, which I was just about able to get down my throat.

After school, everyone would congregate in a local ice cream café and smoke endless cigarettes. Amazingly, smoking was allowed in the school playground in a designated area, this being a convention in Germany that only died out a couple of decades ago.

One of the main reasons for the lack of necessity to exert strong discipline was the system that meant your grades over the course of the school year were absolutely crucial to your progress and success. This was the basis of the system of *"Sitzenbleiben"*, whereby if your average mark at the end of the year wasn't good enough, you had to repeat the year. This concentrated the mind dramatically. If you were failing to pay attention, you'd be unlikely to learn properly and therefore the danger of *"Sitzenbleiben"* increased.

The incredible feeling of general kindness and open-mindedness that prevailed in that school was emphasized when I was invited to go with one of the classes on a *"Klassenfahrt"*. This is something that happens in Germany, and works incredibly well as a bonding activity. The entire class decamps for a week to some picturesque and historic part of the country and stays in a youth hostel.

I was to learn a great deal more about the German school system when, as an adult, I went and worked there for three years, but that blissful month in 1965 exposed me to a German society that was effectively classless. Everyone went to a good quality school, they all mixed with each other, people's social class or level of wealth were of no relevance and they all ended up having very similar and equally civilized life chances. It had an enormous effect on the attitude I would take socially for the rest of my life.

(x.) Moving On

For someone who had been marked down as a potential academic high achiever at the age of 11, my eventual exam results were a disgrace. At O-level, I got top grades in the three subjects I was good at and enjoyed: English, French and German. All the rest of the results were mediocre, apart from Latin, geography and history, all of which I failed. I duly re-took all three and failed them again. In history, I even managed to get a lower grade than I had at the first attempt. Naturally, my father was devastated.

A-levels were little better, because I was going through my "couldn't-care-less" days. I didn't work hard enough, wasn't gifted enough and ended up with three Bs. This was when things went even more wrong than they already had with my education. The idiotic Goofus suggested that I should take something called S-levels. My father was desperate for me to get into Cambridge and it was supposed that the S-levels would improve my chances. I realised later that neither of them had any idea what S-levels were, or what they entailed.

It wasn't until I had been actually entered for these exams that it was discovered that, in order to take them, I had to re-take my A-levels. This was a frustrating and futile activity, which resulted in no improvement, as I again ended up with Bs. On top of that, S-levels were way out of my academic and intellectual reach, plus the school had no tradition of teaching for them and didn't know the criteria. Perhaps if I had been at a top institution like Eton or Harrow, I might have had a chance. As it was, it was verging on cruel to make me go through it, and I think even my father eventually realised that his ambitions had taken him a step too far.

He himself had attended Jesus College, Cambridge and, for some reason, he thought that the fact that he knew various people who worked there would help me to get in. In fact, it turned out that he had no influence at all, and I had to go through a most humiliating procedure, involving travelling to Cambridge and taking some entrance exams. I was humbled and made to feel completely insignificant, as the examination contained questions about topics that I had never tackled or even been aware of. I had to hand in an empty sheet.

When I therefore came to apply for other universities, my criteria were vague and misconceived, because the headmaster suggested that I apply for both Oxford and Cambridge. I later discovered that, if you apply for one, the other won't consider you. For Number 3, I put Bristol, simply because it was the nearest city to where I grew up and I quite liked it. I again found out later that Bristol didn't like being put third on the bill after Oxbridge. Then came the University of East Anglia, which I chose because it was in Norwich, near to Ipswich, where my father had been educated. Southampton I chose because I'd once visited the city with my brother-in-law and thought it had a nice park. Last on the list came Durham, another foolish choice, as it, too, was a "posh" university that didn't like to be listed below others.

With my dodgy selection of Bs, I was naturally rejected by all of them except UEA. Nevertheless, UEA did turn out to be the most spectacularly fine choice, even though I was approaching the institution from a position of total ignorance. UEA was one of a bunch of "new" universities like Essex, Kent and Sussex, which were progressive and non-stuffy. Founded in 1963, it was famous for the Zig-zag brutalist concrete buildings, designed by Denys Lasdun and situated on something called the University Plain, on the outskirts of Norwich. In fact, even by the time I got there in 1968, the main buildings still hadn't been completed, and much of the activity went on in something called the University Village, which was a collection of prefabricated constructions about a mile away.

Chapter 2
THE UNI-VERSAL

(i.) Agri-Culture

Before I packed my trunk and headed for Norwich to commence real adult life, I had another kind of educational experience to go through. My middle sister had recently married a gentlemen called Colin, who was a farm manager. In need of some cash and something to occupy me during the long summer holidays, I asked if I could have a job on his farm. Thus began a series of farming experiences that lasted for the following five summers. Here, I learnt a huge amount about the meaning of work. I knew absolutely nothing about the practicalities of manual labour but, unbeknown to them, the workers there gave me a deep educational experience, as they taught me about tractor-driving and all the associated skills such as using power take-offs and oil-operated lifting gear, as well as assorted highly dangerous and sophisticated implements, such as rotavators, seed drills and foreloaders.

All my rote learning of kings, queens, grammatical structures, geographical concepts and mathematical theorems added up to precisely nothing in this environment, and the workers were absolutely scornful of my pathetic ignorance and lack of skills. Because this was their field of expertise and they had experienced nothing else, they had never before come across someone so ignorant. They rolled their eyes and sneered in utter contempt. This was where I learnt a very important lesson about fellow human beings. These guys, mainly middle-aged or older, had had virtually zero education, having left school, like my mother, at the age of fourteen, but they had no need of the kind of education I had been gifted.

I was in awe at the incredible skills they displayed, ploughing fields with millimetre precision and expertly repairing the equipment when it broke down. They worked massively long hours for very low pay, but eventually, I earned their trust by simply throwing myself on their mercy, admitting my abject uselessness and begging them to teach me. It turned out that, once they had grasped the concept that there were people who weren't as skilled as them, they developed some patience and took pleasure in instructing me. I can't say I ever ended up enjoying the work, but I was aware that my education had been broadened in a significant way.

Once again, the path to socialism had opened up, as I wrestled with the concept that these guys, who had so much to contribute, would be largely viewed by mainstream society as ignorant manual workers and thus valued less highly. "This can't possibly continue long-term," I thought. "Things will surely change," but I'm writing this in the era of the "gig economy", where people's skills and hard work tend to be punished rather than rewarded.

(i.) East Anglicanism

Accommodation at UEA took the form of an old RAF station at Fifer's Lane on the edge of Norwich. The barracks-like buildings were at least warm, comfortable and clean. Indeed, we even had a posse of cleaners who came round and dusted our rooms and made our beds every morning. Why we were deemed incapable of doing this ourselves I don't know, but I always enjoyed nattering to the cleaners. I even ended up with a single room after two false starts in a double one. My first co-habitant turned out to be a gay person, who declared within the first week that he fancied me. After a brief discussion, we agreed that it was a situation that wasn't really suitable for either of us, so he was replaced by a great guy from Kuwait, who was extremely studious. Within a few days, he had complained to the administrators that my late-night drinking and playing of music was spoiling his studies.

I made friends quickly in this environment, because there were communal kitchens and socialising areas. Prominent among my fellow first-year students was a bunch of highly intelligent, super-smart lads from Liverpool. I had never even heard a Scouse accent in my life, but I immediately took to them. I wasn't intimidated by their working class background, but was thrilled by their fierce intellectual sharpness and deep knowledge of politics and culture. All of them had been to various state grammar schools in the Liverpool area, and they were mainly doing Social Studies. This was a concept of which I had never heard. In fact, my school education had given me no knowledge of the existence of society, apart from telling us that we shouldn't associate with people from state schools. I simply was incapable of keeping up with those guys, several of whom went on to attain first-class degrees and to have successful academic and political careers.

The course I had selected was European Studies. This offered the chance to specialise in one language, in my case German, and to explore it from a wider angle than simply linguistics and literature. The first year was occupied by something called "Prelims", a preliminary course lasting a couple of terms, in which you were invited to dip your toe into a range of subject areas, before deciding what you were going to concentrate on for the rest of the course. It was a four-year course, the third of which was to be spent in the country of the language of your choice.

Coming from such a restricted educational background, it was exciting to be introduced to subjects such as philosophy and semantics. I was exactly at the age when it was suitable to ruminate on the musings of Descartes and Voltaire, that baffling stuff about trees falling in woods and whether a table really was a table. Our philosophy teacher was a strange young man who, as he spoke, crawled around the tables and window sills of the seminar room, rather like Spider-Man. We loved his eccentricity, without understanding much of what he was saying, until a headline in the Eastern Daily Press revealed that had been caught in the middle of the night stealing drugs from the university pharmacy, arrested and fired.

Two young lecturers taught us inspiringly about aspects of linguistics, a field which has held enormous interest for me ever since. Most pleasingly, there was a module on modern history, and all of a sudden, I discovered that there was more to history than learning dates by heart. Concentrating on the first and second world wars, we delved into the whys and wherefores of how these conflicts developed. The only problem was that the lectures were held in a gigantic lecture hall, stuffed with hundreds of students. One particular professor created an interesting scene in that room, because he had a nervous habit which meant that he smiled all the time, even when there was nothing to smile about. Smiling, like yawning, is infectious and, as you looked around, you could see wall-to-wall people grinning all over their faces, while learning about extremely depressing, violent and brutal events.

The initial Prelim period was quite hard work, because it was compulsory to attend sessions, and at the end of it there were exams, which would determine whether you were allowed to continue the course. As I was enjoying myself so much, I made sure to do just enough work to pass the Prelims. The Prelim period was very good for me, because it was quite highly structured and helped bridge the gap between the iron rule of school and the more voluntary discipline required at further education level.

It was after the end of the Prelims that the wheels came off my university education. Now one was supposed to be far more self-sufficient and willing to do original research. In practice, because of the "newness" of the institution, there were very few checks on what we were actually doing. For my second year in Norwich, there were only a couple of seminars each week and the amount of work we had to hand in was tiny, just a few essays a term. Rather than go to the library and do proper research, I tended to regurgitate A-level style work and invariably received mediocre grades and comments such as "This is more like a sixth-form essay than a university one".

I was never going to shine particularly in higher education, because I lacked motivation and, frankly, wasn't bright enough. Instead, I threw myself into working on the social committee and putting on music gigs, while getting by on the bare minimum in my actual course. I would argue strongly, though, that the skills I learned by being involved in music promotion were an education in themselves, and indeed have served me well ever since. Considering how conservative my father was, it was astonishing that he repeatedly said that he wanted me to go to university for the life experience more than the academic attainment. I took those words perhaps more literally than he would have liked, but I will always be grateful to him nonetheless.

Most of the lecturers at UEA were young and quite dynamic. This caused one or two problems, when numerous cases occurred of staff having affairs with students. One of my friends had to be dissuaded from leaping off the roof of one of the buildings, when he discovered that his girlfriend was having a sexual relationship with her English tutor. I won't elaborate, because the tutor went on to become world famous. The general vibe on campus was pretty much as you would have imagined it to be in the Swinging Sixties. "Free love" was the norm, because access to the contraceptive pill was easy. The "Love and Peace" hippie era was in full swing.

Without appreciating it, we were in an incredibly privileged position, with full maintenance grants, little in the way of anyone checking whether we were doing any work, and a delightfully cheap cost of living. On a Friday, I would go to the student bar with a pound note in my pocket. That was sufficient for seven pints of Watney's Red Barrel at two shillings a pint, a pack of twenty Number 6 cigarettes and a couple of packets of cheese and onion crisps.

In the second year, when we were allowed to choose our own courses, I selected mainly literary offerings. I have to admit that I remember little of any of the content, apart from one seminar that was called "Vienna and Prague At The Turn Of The Century". This concentrated largely on the works of Kafka and Robert Musil, whose brilliant "The Man Without Qualities" offered me a template for future living. The basic teaching was not to get too hung up on what "might be" in life, because everything could just as well be different. You can be content with what you have. It was back to the farm workers again.

In between interviewing various musicians for the student magazine, I also continued the habit of torturing myself by taking part in amateur dramatics. At the time, I had absolutely no inkling that I was interacting with future superstars when I met and wrote features on Marc Bolan, Pink Floyd, Joe Cocker, Jeff Lynne and scores more. The dramatic efforts were considerably less successful, as my panic attacks continued to debilitate me. Nonetheless, I once again found that it was possible to educate yourself without realising you were doing so. For example, by taking a part in Arthur Miller's "The Crucible", I learnt all about the Salem Witch Trials, and by being involved in a play called "Tom Paine", I became aware of the life story of the creator of The Rights Of Man. Astonishingly, Paine had been born in nearby Thetford. The production was directed by Jonny Powell, who later became the Controller of BBC1. My parents came to see this latter performance in the Maddermarket Theatre in Norwich. I felt a warm glow as they both agreed that the avant-garde production was great (even though it wasn't).

Student politics played a major role in daily life, and there was scarcely a time when we were not on strike for some reason or another. At one stage, we were striking because we didn't think the meals in the canteen were good enough. I had several friends who were firebrand communists, so I did my best to study Marx, but gave up in the end, on account of extreme boredom. It was quite simple, though, to sign up to the basics i.e. "all people are equal" and resolve to live life in that way.

(iii.) Kieling Joke

The terms passed quickly, and soon it was time to embark on the much-awaited year abroad. We were allowed to choose anywhere there happened to be a university, so I chose Kiel, in North Germany, because, as a sixth former, I had attended a month-long holiday course there and fallen in love with Schleswig-Holstein. The year I spent in Kiel can be summed up in one word: dossing. There was no requirement to do anything at all. You didn't even have to write a single essay and, what was more, you didn't have to prove that you'd even been there. This was demonstrated by a friend of mine who spent the entire year in Denmark. All you had to do was write the occasional letter to your tutor back in Norwich, saying how you were getting on. This friend would write his letters describing the fictitious seminars he was attending, and send them to me. I would then put them in an envelope, add a stamp and post them to the tutor. *Voilà*.

As for me, I did enrol as a guest student in Kiel and even went to a couple of lectures. Here it became clear that, as had been the case in Norwich, these were mass events with hundreds and hundreds of students sitting and taking notes while some boring professor droned on. Winter arrived and, as the weather got more and more cold, I ended up not bothering with the lectures and, instead, spending entire days under the blankets in my freezing hovel of a "*Wohngemeinschaft*". This was the German word for a "commune", a then-currently fashionable euphemism for being cooped up with a load of acquaintances that you didn't like, and having to share filthy bathrooms and kitchens.

It turned out that UEA political life had been very tame indeed compared to that in Kiel. Dominated by two separate branches of communists, the KBW and the DKP, the demos were less "love and peace" and more "blood and guts". Most weekends, there would be lively anti-war demos that would invariably descend into street violence, featuring flying bricks and flaming vehicles. The German university system was quite extraordinary in that, depending on how much money you had, you could stay at university as long as you wanted, until you eventually accumulated enough certificates to allow you to attain your degree (*"Staatsexamen"*). A friend of mine that I lived with in Kiel worked part-time to finance his studies, and took a total of ten years before he did his *"Staatsexamen"* final exams. This was by no means a record.

I am embarrassed to admit that I got into a certain incident in Kiel that bordered on illegality, in fact crossed the border. I was approached by a mature student who had been studying English for many years with little success, probably associated with the fact that he was a gambling addict. Initially Gunter (which was his name) told me he wanted private language tuition. He offered me way above the going rate, so of course, I accepted with alacrity. After the third session, he said that there was something he wanted to talk to me about, as he had decided I was trustworthy, and described the following scenario:

In a month's time, he was to sit an important exam, which would clear the way for him to achieve his *"Staatsexamen"*. Unfortunately, he had no confidence that he would be able to pass the exam and wondered if I would be willing to assist? He described the plan. He would go into the exam, which was due to last five hours. In the first half an hour or so, he would transcribe the questions, excuse himself to go to the toilet, then pass the questions into the next cubicle, where his friend /accomplice was waiting. The accomplice would then mount his motorbike and ride to Gunter's flat, where I would be waiting, pen poised. I would then have around three hours in which to write the responses.

We actually had a practice run to demonstrate how long it would take him to transcribe my efforts. As it transpired, it all worked like a dream. Gunter ended up with a very good mark and, as far as I'm aware, went on to a career in English teaching. It might possibly explain why so many English teachers in Germany can barely string a sentence together. Writing this now makes my flesh creep, because I did it purely for money. Gunter had plenty of wealth and was more than willing to give some of it to me in order to achieve his goal.

Being hopelessly broke, I advertised in the local paper for some more private pupils, and embarked on English tuition in the evenings. This gave me a lifelong dislike of one-to-one teaching. Especially when working with adults, it can be extremely intense, and an hour can seem to drag on forever. The motivation of people to seek tutoring is sometimes unclear. There was one respectable, middle-aged gentleman whom I visited every week for six months in Kiel, who was clearly paying for the lessons simply because he was very lonely. Another couple that signed up seemed incapable of learning anything, and each week, as I tested what they remembered from the previous lesson, I realised that it was absolutely nothing. A third person engaged me because she was trying to write a thesis in English on brain surgery. This was when I discovered that certain specific subject areas have their own vocabulary. I didn't understand a word of the English documents, so our attempts to translate them into German were futile.

(iv.) A Degree Of Separation

Back in Norwich, it was theoretically time to buckle down, do some work and try and get a degree. In practice, none of this happened, because I found myself in a hall of residence occupied by a gang of people who had spent similarly dissolute "years abroad" and, like me, had got into the habit of lazing around. One thing that was very noticeable, though, was the excellence of my spoken German. That applied to everybody who'd spent the year abroad. They all came back speaking their target language very fluently. One guy, who had been in Vienna, came back with an Austrian accent that was so strong that I could scarcely understand a word he said. A female Austrian lecturer, however, was hugely impressed, and they became quite good friends.

The clear fact of the matter was that the year abroad had been a very valuable educational experience for us all, despite the fact that virtually no formal education had taken place at all. I tried hard to do the necessary work, spending some time in the university library. In years 1 and 2, anybody going to the library had been considered to be a swot. I always felt extremely uncomfortable in the library and unable to concentrate. There was too much going on around me and generally, I found it easier to do my essays in all-night sessions, alone in my room, free from distractions.

The time came for the final exams. I was reasonably confident in doing okay in the language sections, but my literary studies had been minimal, simply writing the odd essay on one book by each author. For example, my knowledge of Kafka was limited to the very slim and delightfully surreal "Metamorphosis", rather than tackling some of his considerably longer and more challenging works. This plainly wasn't going to be sufficient but, in what I thought was quite a clever move, I had brought back from Germany some strange little booklets called *"Reklams Romanführer"*. These contained summarized, potted versions of great works of literature, so one could get the gist of them without actually having to read them. This was a particularly attractive option in the case of the works of Thomas Mann, who tended to write enormously long tomes such as "Buddenbrooks", where sentences could last for anything up to half a page.

I still feel guilty and embarrassed about what happened on the day of the literature paper in the final exam. Most of my fellow students in that area were extremely studious females from private school backgrounds, all of whom had dutifully spent their particular "years abroad" actually studying. With trembling fingers, I opened the literature paper, and my terror turned to joy when I saw that the essay titles coincided exactly with the few topics that I had actually revised. Yesss! I was able to scribble away for the allocated three hours and emerged from the examination hall declaring in a loud voice, "Fucking hell, what a jammy bastard I am! All my topics came up, woo hoo!"

The two girls standing next to me both burst into tears. By chance, the topics that had come up were the only ones they hadn't revised. When the upsettingly public list of results was posted on the notice-board a couple of weeks later, the poor ladies concerned ended up with 2-2s, whereas I was awarded an outrageous and completely undeserved 2-1. "An upper second," huffed my father. "That's rather good." He failed to add that, had I gone to Cambridge, I would no doubt have been kicked out, rusticated, masticated or whatever the word was.

In keeping with the spirit of the times, I duly refused to attend the graduation ceremony, but did receive a piece of paper confirming that unmerited "upper second". But what exactly does one do with an "upper second"? I was a classic candidate for the "those who can, do, and those who can't, teach" cliché, because after such a random history of education, I'd ended up in the position where the only thing I could actually do was speak a couple of foreign languages.

(v.) In for the Kiel

Fate intervened here, in the form of a phone call from Ian, the fellow student I mentioned before, who had spent his entire year abroad in Denmark. He had unsurprisingly struck up a relationship there and planned to return during the summer holidays. He would be travelling via Kiel and asked if I fancied coming along with him for the ride. As I had already applied, and been accepted, for teacher training in Bristol, the plan was just for a brief visit, but it didn't turn out that way. Reunited with some of my old pals in the Baltic port, I discovered that they were living in a different, even more filthy and sordid flea, lice, and mice-ridden slum. They cheerfully told me there was a room free there if I fancied moving in?

There was no way I would have accepted this offer, but I visited the *"Lektorat Deutsch für Ausländer"* to say hello to a lecturer there called Dr Horst Zindler. We had first met when doing a German summer course that Father sent me on at the age of 17. During my year abroad, I had occasionally attended evening sessions in this department of the university, which existed in order to teach German language skills to foreign students who needed help in that area.

Dr Zindler now asked me if I'd be interested in helping them with some research they were doing on "interference". "Interference" is when a person's mother tongue "interferes" with their learning of a foreign language, causing them to construct sentences in unusual ways and misuse vocabulary. As part of their research, they were engaging people with various mother tongues to examine essays written by people in German, and analyse which mistakes were caused by interference, and which were not. The results would presumably help them to target certain language teaching techniques to specific candidates.

I pricked up my ears when Dr Zindler said that there would be a small fee involved, if I were willing to do research for one day a week. I hesitated, because even the slum I would potentially be occupying wouldn't be cheap. Noticing my doubts, Dr Zindler said that he would make an enquiry with the university's English department to see if they needed any assistance. The very next day, I was summoned to the English department, where I spoke to the editor of a learned literary magazine called *"Literatur In Wissenschaft und Unterricht"*, and was offered a post as a so-called *"Wissenschaftliche Hilfskraft"*.

This was pretty much the lowest-of-the-low in academic circles, but it potentially was a job of sorts. It was 500 Marks a month for working mornings only, which would cover the rent. It was still summer and in Kiel, the weather was beautiful. The beaches beckoned, Dr Zindler took me out on his boat on the Baltic and, before I knew it, I had written to Bristol University, postponing my PGCE course.

I had just about enough to live on, but the living conditions were off-the-scale horrible and from a career point of view, I was going absolutely nowhere. The job in the English department entailed doing very odd things. I worked in the same office as a young couple who were very kind, but led an extraordinary life of elite academia. For a project they were working on, they had engaged a press cuttings company to identify pieces of English drama that were being performed in public in Germany. Every week, I would receive a large envelope of press cuttings, and my job was to cut them out and stick them in a kind of scrapbook, keeping a note of the dates and places. This was an enjoyable and simple procedure.

Meanwhile, I was also in charge of the duplicating processes in the department. Every day, various lecturers came to me with tests and worksheets they had created, to be run off on something called a Banda machine. These infernal devices were common at the time, and enabled the production of large quantities of papers to be distributed to students. Inside a steel barrel were some very smelly liquid chemicals, which enabled blue ink to be processed onto slightly soggy paper. I was convinced that this stuff was making me high, because it had such a pungent chemical smell, and I would feel really quite drowsy, standing there for hours at a time, getting repetitive strain from turning the handle on the machine. There was also another, much more sophisticated device, that enabled typewritten sheets to be run off. It was constantly breaking down, and I had several miserable incidents where the carefully-crafted worksheets simply disintegrated, much to the fury of the lecturers who had brought them to me.

Every now and again, I would get ideas above my station and try to drop a hint that I would like to be doing something a little bit more challenging. I wrote a few articles for the LWU magazine, but they were all rapidly rejected. Nonetheless, it has to be said that this job was useful when trailing around the city's nightclubs in the evenings. I could make new friends and acquaintances by casually dropping the line that I was working in the university. You could see that they were thinking that I must be some kind of lecturer or academic. Little did they know the truth, although my clothes probably stank of the pungent Banda fluid.

In order to try and liven things up a bit, I decided to confront my phobia and get involved in a drama production. This time, however, I was to be the producer, and the actors were to be various well-disposed and keen students from the university's English department. I found a one-act play, originally written for radio, called "The Object", and we set to work to rehearse in a futuristic building at the centre of the university campus. After a few months, we eventually presented the play for a three-day run to small but enthusiastic audiences. I'd learnt the lesson that I was more suited to working behind the scenes than in the public eye. There was a lukewarm review in the local press and I actually got to glue it into the album in the office.

Meanwhile, I was getting stuck into the other job, which consisted of identifying the kinds of mistakes that were being made by English-speaking students in their German essays. I spotted certain categories and classified the various errors according to their likely causes. This actually was an interesting and entertaining activity and, after a few months, I had accumulated nearly a hundred pages of examples and theories. The only problem was that it was all in longhand, and I was the world's slowest typist. It turned out that the leading lady in "The Object", with whom I had become quite close, had taken a typing course. So, for a small cut of my wages, she was able to type it all out for me. Eventually, it was inserted into a folder and presumably put onto a shelf, never to be consulted again.

Before setting off back to the UK to start teacher training in Bristol, I sent a copy of this document to Colin Good, my old tutor from UEA. To my great surprise, he wrote back saying that, if I had stayed on to do a PhD (something which had never crossed my mind for a second), my research would have been sufficient to qualify me for a doctorate. Just think, I could have been a Doctor. But would I have been happy? Who knows?

(vi.) Bristol Fashion

The year in Bristol was a very hard and challenging period. Once again, I was living in squalid conditions, but pretty much from the first day I felt inspired and highly motivated by the course. Yes, it is true that those who can't do anything usually end up teaching, but I think I am one of the many who start off for that reason, but end up discovering that their vocation is indeed to be teaching. It was just that, up until then, I hadn't been aware of it.

Bristol University's education department had a strong reputation in the foreign languages field. Its status was built on the talents of two young lecturers called John and Herbert, who worked in tandem to indoctrinate us with a particular teaching technique to which they were passionately committed. Following on from, and retaining elements of, a previous system called the Communicative Method, it was called Audio-Visual Teaching. It had only recently been introduced as a way of utilising the first baby-steps of technology, which were tape recorders and slide projectors. I will describe later in more detail exactly how this technique worked, but the basic principle was relatively simple. To learn a language, you have to first listen, then speak, then read and finally write. If you do this, your pronunciation is less likely to be interfered with by learning from the written page. It was so far from how I had been taught, i.e. copying stuff from the blackboard and hardly ever speaking, that one needed a huge adjustment in attitude to accept it.

The way that they converted all of us on the very first day was brilliantly simple. They divided us into small groups to have a session in a language that none of us had ever encountered before. There were groups doing Polish, Dutch and Italian, each with a native speaker doing the presentation. After two hours in the Italian group, I was astounded to find that I was able to hold a basic conversation in Italian without having read or written a word. Within less than a day, I had become a passionate advocate for this system of language teaching, which I had never even heard of before.

Once we had mastered the techniques, which contained little grammar and concentrated on language to be used in everyday situations, we were encouraged to start creating our own resources, by going into a studio and making recordings, as well as into a photo lab to manufacture appropriate slides. My girlfriend Rosamund, now also living in Bristol, helped with this, as she was an accomplished artist.

The middle term of the course was devoted to teaching practice. This was where the clash between theory and reality started to dampen my enthusiasm slightly, because, basically, we were just hurled straight into the classroom, with very little practical knowledge of how to deal with reluctant and difficult kids. Every day, I would ride my extremely unreliable and dangerous scooter out to Hengrove School, a comprehensive in the suburbs of Bristol. I can't say it was a very fine example of a British educational establishment. Discipline was shaky to say the least, staff largely demoralised and the clientèle pretty rough and uninterested.

Coming into this environment, full of enthusiasm, committed to a particular teaching technique and determined to see it succeed, led to some major disappointments, as I struggled with the slide projector and the tape recorder and tried to make sense of a rather passé and not particularly inspiring French course called Longman's Audio-Visual French. I would reach the evenings completely exhausted, and was forced to dedicate myself to planning lessons literally minute-by-minute, so that there was no chance of losing control either of the teaching programme, or the pupils.

I do remember one occasion when I came close to quitting. The deputy head was one of those bristly-moustached ex-army types, whose main job was to bawl at recalcitrant teenagers. During one particular lesson, I finally lost patience with a particular boy who wouldn't stop talking and messing about. In my childhood school, sending someone out of the classroom to cool down had been perfectly normal, so I told the boy to go and stand outside in the corridor for five minutes. My plan was to invite him back in shortly afterwards. Unfortunately, old bristly-moustache had been patrolling nearby. Discovering what was going on, he grabbed the boy by the neck, yanked him back into the classroom and, in full view of all the pupils, gave me a massive telling-off, accusing me of undermining the discipline of the school by allowing children to wander the corridors unsupervised.

This act of arch unprofessionalism (his, not mine, I thought) frightened the living daylights out of me, as I feared that I was about to be fired for insubordination. Luckily, it was almost the end of term and I was able to escape the torture chamber relatively unscathed, but it did engender some doubts about whether I was cut out for the teaching profession after all.

These doubts weren't greatly helped by the project that I became involved with in the final term of the year. In quite a high-profile study, that later developed into several academic books, some lecturers in the English department were doing some research called "Young Teachers And Reluctant Learners". Bristol was considered a good spot for this, as the city was awash with naïve, youthful potential pedagogues and kids who had attention issues. I entered this very altruistically, on the basis that I wanted to help out the most deprived children, but it was extremely intense and difficult work. It involved us associating closely with families who were suffering from relationship breakdowns, alcoholism, drug addiction and violence, and assessing the impact on their secondary schooling. To my surprise and pleasure, I ended up really enjoying the work and became quite good friends with a couple of kids and their dysfunctional families.

By the end of the year, sparked by my new-found enthusiasm for language teaching, my work ethic had developed into something contrasting dramatically with anything that had gone before. I felt I deserved my teaching certificate when I received it, but I was unable to quell the hankering I had for living and working in Germany. This led to a sequence of events that were to define the entire rest of my adult life.

Chapter 3
GYM PRACTICE

(i.) Those Who Can, Do...

Leafing through the voluminous Jobs section of the Times Educational Supplement, I came upon an advert seeking graduates to be employed, teaching English in Germany. Most countries experience teacher shortages from time to time, and that was currently happening in Germany. There weren't enough teachers of English to fill all the available posts. A private company called "The Centre For British Teachers In Europe" had been set up, in order to recruit staff and allocate them round the various parts of Germany that needed help. Looking at the various unattractive parts of the UK where German teaching jobs were on offer, it was a no-brainer for me to be tempted to return to the country where I felt more comfortable.

You didn't have any choice in where you went; once you had been accepted, you simply got posted to a particular school. I was extremely lucky to be sent to a beautiful but also very lively city in northern Germany called Bremen. I had scarcely heard of it, and certainly never been there, but

I was full of optimism as I set sail aboard the usual ghastly DFDS ferry full of drunken squaddies, heading for Hamburg, where the induction course was to take place. There, in a large house in a smart suburb called Rissen, I met up with the motley collection of pedagogues who had taken up the challenge. Some, although not many, were linguists like me. The majority of them were teachers of English As A Foreign Language and came from various English-speaking countries such as South Africa and New Zealand.

Although in many respects I ended up being quite critical of the Centre For British Teachers, the two-week induction course was in fact very comprehensive and helpful. It needed to be, because the German school system was very different from either my private school education or my Teaching Practice experience. Among the things we had to learn was the marking system for the all-important *"Klassenarbeiten"* (class tests), which were the only way of assessing progress. It was clear that accurate and fair marking was a crucial element. We were also instructed in the kind of teaching techniques that would be expected in a German school. These were very traditional methods, such as translation, précis and grammar exercises, and therefore not remotely similar to what I had been taught just a few months before. However, being a bit of a grammar nerd, I looked forward to trying my best to combine traditional and modern teaching methods.

You know when you look back on life and remember certain days that were absolutely crucial turning points (or *"Wendepunkte"*, as I had learnt in literature sessions at UEA)? It was 7am, and I was in a *"Stehcafé"*, an establishment where you stand and drink coffee. Bremen had a strong focus on coffee, being the headquarters of both Tchibo and Eduscho, the two biggest coffee companies. Germans love their coffee, and they love it strong. The whole city smelt of a mixture of coffee roasting and tobacco, because the other main industry at the time, apart from shipping, was the cigarette company HB. HB stands for "Hansestadt Bremen", so-called because of the city's rôle at the heart of the Hanseatic League in the thirteenth and fourteenth centuries, along with other ports such as Lübeck and Hamburg. In that café, I was indulging in those two products, namely very strong black coffee and a HB cigarette.

Lessons were due to start at 7.45, and I aimed to get to the school at 7.30. I hadn't even visited the school before and only knew how to get there from looking at a map and choosing a particular tram route. In less than half an hour, I was expected to walk into a classroom and start teaching English. I was completely on my own; there was no support system, and for the first time in my life, I had to take serious responsibility and - as they say - step up to the plate. It was absolutely terrifying. I stood there, shaking from the adrenaline encouraged by the bitter coffee, sweating from the nicotine coursing through my veins, and my head spinning in circles. If it had been feasible to get back on the tram and chicken out, I'd have done it.

The "*Gymnasium Waller Ring*", when I found it, was a huge, ugly, dark, old, intimidating-looking building, more like a prison than an educational establishment. It was situated in a poor area of town, surrounded by the industrial landscape of the harbour. There was no greenery for miles and the playground was a bleak, asphalted area, where the pupils huddled in groups and smoked. Inside, the picture was exactly as you would expect an old-fashioned school to be: dark, echoing corridors with doors leading off them into traditional, formal classrooms.

I had received my timetable by post and been rather bamboozled to see that it consisted of five Year 11 classes and nothing else. I later discovered that they had been allocated to me because it was considered to be the place where, if I was a disaster as a teacher, I would be able to wreak the least damage. Faced with five lessons to five parallel classes on the first day, I decided to do a general introduction, telling them a bit about myself, and then inviting the pupils to do the same to me in English. I planned to conduct all the lessons using only English, which I had learnt on the induction course was the convention. I entered the first class, shaking from head to foot, and launched into my prepared activities. The pupils were aged 16 and 17, both sexes dressed mainly in jeans, t-shirts and parkas, the boys all with long hair and the beginnings of moustaches.

Immediately, I was struck by the very high quality of the responses. All of them had been learning English for six years, so I suppose it wasn't surprising. Year 11, or the *"elfte Klasse"* in German, was the first year in the top section of the school, the equivalent of the Lower Sixth. The final class in the school was the 13th year, in which pupils took their *"Abitur"*, or A-levels. It was thus considered that, if everything went wrong with my efforts, another teacher would be able to step in and rescue things in years 12 and 13.

The deputy head of the school was also an English teacher, and was in charge of the day-to-day administration of the school, timetabling etc. In the afternoon, I also got to meet the Head of English. He was a very nervous gentleman who, I think, was intimidated by having a native speaker suddenly turning up on his doorstep. He kept emphasizing very clearly that he didn't have the same responsibilities as an English Head of Department; he was merely the senior English teacher. This man, Wolf Lingstädt, kindly invited me to his house several times in the first couple of weeks, to teach me more details of the marking method for *"Klassenarbeiten"*.

I soon discovered that one of the class teachers had announced to his pupils that, not only did I not speak a single word of German, but that I was also engaged to an English girl. I used the first fiction to my advantage by pretending for several weeks that I couldn't speak German. This provided the advantage of allowing me to understand what pupils were saying unguardedly, thinking that I wouldn't understand. Luckily, they were mainly saying nice things. The other matter wasn't strictly true either. I had been semi-officially engaged, I suppose, to my girlfriend Rosamund from school days, with whom I had spent the year in Bristol. She had come out to Germany at the same time as me, to work in a Forces primary school in nearby Fallingbostel. After a short period of time, she hooked up with a soldier and unceremoniously dumped me.

(ii.) Tag für Tag

It wasn't long before I became accustomed to a very different type of school life. Almost all the unnecessary, time-consuming, non-academic aspects of English schools were delightfully absent. There was, of course, no uniform, and scarcely any rules either, because these grammar-school pupils were, in the main, hard-working and highly motivated. Lessons took place only in the mornings, but started at a horribly early hour, and also happened on Saturday mornings. I was to teach a grand total of 20 lessons a week, roughly half of what I would have had to do in the UK. When I wasn't actually teaching, I had no need to be in the school. I was always finished by just after midday and was able to go home for the afternoon nap that all teachers in Germany enjoy. I would then spend the evenings doing preparation and marking homework.

Along with Mike Caldon, a colleague of mine from the Centre For British Teachers, who was working in another Bremen school, we had the idea that we would demonstrate the British education system by introducing certain aspects of it. I therefore made a habit of setting homework and, to the students' amazement, collecting it in, taking it home and marking it. This was something none of my German colleagues would ever have dreamt of doing. The only things that were marked were the all-important précis-type *"Klassenarbeiten"* that took place three times a term, each test lasting an entire morning.

The lack of compulsion to be in school applied to the pupils as well. If they had a free lesson, either in the timetable or caused by teacher absence, they were free to go outside the school, wander round, go for a drink in a café etc, as had been the case in Schöningen. There were no school meals and the only sustenance provided was the milk and cocoa that still remained a tradition.

A challenge that I had to rise to in the first few weeks was what exactly to teach, because there was no textbook to follow and no actual guidelines as to what the content of the lessons should be. I had acquired a superb book by a UK writer called Robert O'Neill, entitled "English In Situations". This I used constantly, because the material offered in it provided a basis for conversation, grammar and discussion topics. Built around this, I spent many hours researching and creating reading resources, grammar and writing activities and other such ways of filling the time.

O'Neill had invented a tool called a Substitution Drill, a technique which I found incredibly useful and employed almost every day, at every level. A Substitution Drill is a devastatingly simple activity that forces learners to manipulate the language. It needs to be carried out at quite some speed, for spontaneity and concentration, almost like a quick-fire quiz. Here's a simple example: The teacher starts with a short sentence and then adds a series of prompts:

Initial sentence: The woman walks down the road.

Prompt: along

Response: The woman walks along the road .

Prompt: is walking

Response: The woman is walking along the road.

Prompt: dog

Response: The dog is walking along the road.

Prompt: running

Response: The dog is running along the road.

Prompt: was

Response: The dog was running along the road.

Prompt: would be

Response: The dog would be running along the road.

Prompt: would have been

Response: The dog would have been running along the road.

Prompt: not

Response: The dog would not have been running along the road.

Prompt: should

Response: The dog should not have been running along the road.

… etc, etc, as long as you want to keep going, and depending on what point you want to practise.

Classes were divided into two streams: the so-called Language Branch and the Science Branch. English was compulsory for everybody until *"Abitur"* level, but those in the Language Branch were expected to achieve higher standards. This meant that there were variations of language ability among the different classes. The average class size was around 25, although a couple of classes had as few as fifteen people in them. I remember very clearly one particular Science Branch class, because the lessons took place in a tiny room on the very top floor of the huge building at 7:45 am on a Saturday morning. We didn't get much done, as pretty much everyone, including me, was slightly hung-over.

The atmosphere, however, was almost exactly the same as at the Schöningen *"Gymnasium"* all those years before: laid-back and friendly. At the end of the first week, I was approached by a pupil, called Volker, who explained that he and his friends had come up with an idea and wondered what I would think of it? The plan was that we should gather a small group of students, go somewhere on a Saturday evening, have a few drinks and something to eat and talk English the entire time. They christened these get-togethers *"Groschen-Fête"*. A *"Groschen"* was a ten-Pfennig piece and the system was that, if you were ever stuck for vocabulary and needed to ask the meaning of a word, or, indeed, if you inadvertently spoke in German, you had to put a *"Groschen"* into a pot. The accumulated money would then be used to purchase beer for the next session. I consulted Wolf Lingstädt about whether meeting pupils socially would be acceptable?

"Why not?" he replied. "They are grown-ups, they're responsible, they're allowed to drink beer and all they are planning to do is improve the standard of their English. Go for it."

Thus began a tradition which lasted a couple of years and, in fact, on the very first Saturday, they all came to my very primitive and uncomfortable bedsit, ate baked potatoes (which I had prepared as an English tradition), spoke English all evening and generally had a great time. All of them are now lifetime friends of mine, with whom I am still in touch nearly fifty years later. I was a young teacher, they were mature sixth formers and, although it might have been frowned on in the UK, there it certainly wasn't. The age difference wasn't great enough to create a social barrier.

For staff and students to interact like this was considered quite normal. A good colleague on the staff produced plays in English, and the post-rehearsal socializing was an integral part of the process. I helped him direct an English performance of the play "The Matchmaker", on which the musical "Hello Dolly" had been based. They even persuaded me to have a small walk-on part, playing a waiter. I had just one line, but still suffered crippling stage fright, although it never crossed my mind that it could be a sign of compromised mental health.

There were several young members of staff who regularly partied with the students, and I was invited to quite a few of the events. Some staff members and students were members of the two communist parties, the KBW and the DKP. As politically-minded people do, a major part of the get-togethers consisted of deep discussions, or, as the Germans like to call it, "*diskutieren*". If you, as a teacher, were considered politically conservative, you were unlikely to be popular, but luckily, I wore my socialist ideals on my sleeve (although I never joined any political party) and was generally given the thumbs-up.

It sounds awfully smug to say it, but it's true: I was popular as a teacher. I was young enough to be into the same fashions, music and culture as the students, but the most important fact was a simple one: I was English. This gave me the curiosity factor, but also an instant advantage, because being English was cool, admirable and welcomed. In today's dismal post-Brexit times, this seems scarcely believable, but I benefited from it big-time. I soon learnt how to exploit this goodwill to help raise the language standards of my classes by encouraging *"diskutieren"* in English, selecting issue-based texts that encouraged students to join in. Added to that, I introduced elements that few German teachers would have considered useful in their teaching: jokes, competitions, games and, above all, songs. My rudimentary few chords on the guitar enabled me to perform politically meaningful songs by the likes of Bob Dylan, Woody Guthrie and Pete Seeger.

There were some oddball characters among the staff. Two of the male teachers were called Meyer, *Mathe-Meyer* and *Englisch-Meyer*. Englisch-Meyer invited me out during my first week, saying he wanted to introduce me to Bremen's night-life. He took me to the dodgy train station area and into some seedy strip clubs there, where he tried to persuade me to join him the following weekend at the casinos in nearby Travemünde. Even I could see that these activities would be the road to ruin, so I declined. Some time later, he asked me to be godfather to his baby boy, although I hardly knew him. I'm embarrassed to say I wasn't a good godfather and we lost touch.

There was a seedy old French teacher whose nickname was *"Geier"*, meaning "Vulture". He had the reputation of letching after the teenage girls, and legend had it that his trick was to drop his car keys down the cleavage of girls during lessons, and then reach in and take them out again. This was presented as truth but I can't believe that, even in that relaxed environment, he would have got away with it. He was the only teacher who was really unpopular. Almost all the staff were outstandingly professional and gifted, providing a solid, perhaps not very inspiring, but high quality education.

One member of staff the pupils warned me about straight away was called Herr Illmann. For some reason, he doubled up his teaching career with a parallel venture as a used car salesman. "Watch out for him, he will try and sell you a crap car", I was warned, and indeed, within the first two weeks, he took me aside in the staff room and told me about a Volkswagen Beetle he had for a bargain price, that he said would be ideal for me. Fool that I was, I fell for it, and ended up with a highly fallible vehicle that let me down almost constantly. It spent far more time in the local mechanic's workshop than actually functioning on the road. This of course caused much hilarity among my little gang of *"Groschenfête"* pupils.

This charming bunch got me into a couple of scrapes. My initial bed-sit was highly unsuitable, so I located a one-bedroom flat in a nicer part of town. It was unfurnished but, in the local newspaper, I spotted an advert for some furniture being offered for sale cheaply by someone who was moving house. Excellent! But how was I to get the furniture from there to the flat? Sensing a good day out and a bit of a laugh, Volker and his mates volunteered to carry it for me, and Bremen city centre was treated to the extraordinary sight of me, as a kind of Pied Piper, leading a procession of about ten teenagers lugging mattresses, bookcases and chairs.

To add to these basics, I went to a department store in the city centre and ordered two easy chairs. The previous removal having been such a success, the pupils volunteered to collect these for me as well. It seemed a good idea, until they arrived at my flat carrying three of them, instead of the two that I had paid for. They charmingly assumed that I would be delighted by this bonus, and encouraged me just to hang onto the extra one. For months, I tiptoed past the store, which lay on my daily route to school, just in case anybody should identify me as the phantom chair thief.

At Waller Ring, I learnt the importance of quality senior management in a school. The Headmaster, Herr Mumme, was a delightful gentleman with an air of natural authority and deep kindness, a definite father-figure who was regarded with great affection by both staff and pupils. The Deputy Head was an English specialist called Dr Hans Brinkmann, who was to end up having a very strong influence on my life. Dr Brinkmann was rather serious, but endlessly patient and helpful to me. He was in charge of the day-to-day running of the school. Each morning, we would study the meticulously neat notes that he would pin up on the notice board to inform us of timetable changes. If anyone was ill, or there was any kind of problem and a lesson had to be cancelled, he merely wrote the magic letters F-A in the timetable box. This stood for "*Fällt aus*", or "cancelled".

The other person I had a lot to do on a day-to-day basis was the janitor, who was called Herr Hammann. To my surprise and pleasure, one of his roles was similar to what I had been doing in Kiel, i.e. operating the Banda machine. If you needed any worksheets run off for a particular lesson, you simply gave them to him and he duplicated them for you.

Neither of the senior managers was responsible for discipline, so there wasn't anyone you could threaten to "send people to". Teachers were viewed as autonomous in their classrooms, and they alone were in charge of the good conduct of their pupils. It soon became gratifyingly clear to me that teachers in Germany were viewed with great respect and admiration, and, incidentally, were remunerated accordingly too. The air of deference with which the parents treated me at the parents' evenings was almost embarrassing, but very welcome.

Because of the crucial importance of the *"Klassenarbeiten"*, I approached the marking of them very conscientiously, following the instructions of Herr Lingstädt to the letter. Mistakes were classified as half mistakes, full mistakes or one-and-a-half mistakes, each marked with red pen in the margin. Much soul-searching and head-scratching went into deciding the severity of each individual mistake, because at the end of the process you had to work out a percentage mark based on a *"Fehlerquozient"*, or "mistake quota". The errors were, in turn, classified into sub-categories such as a grammar mistake, spelling mistake or something called a *"Flüchtigkeitsfehler"*. This meant "careless mistake", and could be a useful catch-all when in doubt.

As the end of the first year approached and the time came to see whether or not pupils would have to repeat the year, detailed examinations of the accuracy of the marking would take place. The marking system went from 1 to 6, with 1 being outstanding and rarely used. 1 to 4 were all classified as a pass, 5 was a fail, which could be compensated for by higher marks in other subjects, and a 6 meant automatic *"sitzenbleiben"*. In my years at Waller Ring, I never issued a single 6, because the consequences would have been so dire for any pupil receiving such a terrible grade.

There were, of course, certain pupils who weren't particularly successful in their essay writing and therefore would have to receive a 5. Then it would kick off in a quiet and pleasingly civilised way in the classroom, as solidarity with fellow students was considered a matter of honour. Endless discussions would take place about the possibility of changing a 5 into a less harmful 4. In cases of extreme doubt, the work would be moderated by another member of staff. In order to attain the correct levels of accuracy in my marking, I would sometimes have to stay up all night, examining intimately the spidery handwriting of various pupils whose grades were in doubt, and agonizing about the severity level of each mistake I was classifying. By the morning, the ashtray on my desk would be overflowing with cigarette ends.

Yes, as was fashionable at the time, I was indeed a heavy smoker. Luckily for me, early in my time at the school, a vote was taken among the staff, and smoking was banned in the staff room. In the interests of democracy, a new place was allocated specifically for smokers, a small room in the cellar. Here, about twenty ostracized staff members were crammed in during break times, and, as might be imagined, the air was appallingly filthy, leading to clothes that reeked of tobacco smoke. This was sufficient to inspire me to quit while the going was good.

In the same week as the *"Raucherkabuff"* was inaugurated, I not only had to attend the compulsory annual chest X-ray, but also chanced upon an article in a magazine that said that, if your lungs were healthy and you quit smoking, it would be only a matter of weeks before your chance of having lung cancer would return to where it would have been if you'd never smoked at all. As the X-ray was clear, I decided to go for it and went cold turkey, from 30 a day, to none. I have a strong memory of sitting in my car, parked outside the main station in Bremen, where I had bought an English newspaper. I suddenly realised that I had emerged from the shop carrying a packet of twenty HB and was about to light up. Horrified at my own behaviour, I screwed up the packet and hurled it into a nearby litter-bin. Since that day, I have never smoked another cigarette, apart from one time when I was extremely drunk in Tobago. But that's another story altogether.

My popularity led to some competition between my five classes as to who would be graced with my presence on the annual "*Klassenfahrt*". In the end, I settled for a Science Branch class which had a particularly entertaining bunch of characters in it. We spent a fantastic week in a youth hostel in Traben-Trarbach on the Mosel, during which I caused much hilarity by joining them in the swimming pool. I was forced to wear the compulsory Speedos and rubber cap, which was insisted upon because my hair was so long. Similar amusement was caused the next year, when we spent a week camping on the North Sea island of Langeoog, where I was required to show my footballing skills in a competition against another school. My abject sporting uselessness was never more exposed than on that day.

At the end of the first year, I got the thumbs up from the authorities and was allowed to continue teaching two of my five classes into year 12. As all of them wanted me to continue teaching them, I was able to select my two favourite classes, but had also requested to be allowed to teach at lower levels, because teaching five parallel classes was hardly very challenging. I therefore took on a year 5 class, a year 8 class and two more year 11s.

My new classes lower down the school brought me enormous joy. I had a year 5 beginners' group and was thrilled to see how receptive, welcoming and charming they were. Their little wide eyes stared up at this strange English person that they had never expected to meet, and they were extremely keen to learn. They loved all the joking and the singing, and joined in everything with alacrity. Most inspiringly for me, the class represented a broad cross-section of society. The school was situated in what could have been seen as a dodgy part of town, yet there was no sign of the social divides caused in the UK by the availability of private schooling. There was no way to discern who came from a more or less wealthy background. It was so fulfilling to work with these highly-motivated children. After just a few months, their English was good enough for us to write and produce a little play called "Mr Bashford". At the end of the year, they presented me with a bound and illustrated written version of the play.

The Year 8 class was a different kettle of fish altogether. They were just reaching that cheeky adolescent age where they wanted to play up, and so were testing my limits. I was absolutely determined to get the best out of these kids, and invested enormous amounts of energy into entertaining them. You had to concentrate for every second and have enough engaging material to retain their attention. That class even tempted me back into drama production, as we put on a one-act crime story called "Murder At One". This was a proper performance in the school hall to a sold-out audience, and involved almost all the pupils in the class in some capacity or other. All this daily input was exhausting, but it was something that was to stand me in good stead in future years of teaching. If you invest a lot of effort into trying to make everything as enjoyable as possible, you will almost always be rewarded by a positive response.

Before long I was tempted, by the offer of money, to start to teach adult evening classes. It's fair to say that the pay and conditions at the secondary school were good enough to leave me with some time and energy on my hands, so it was probably financial greed rather than anything else that motivated me. The lessons went under the label of *"Volkshochschule"* (People's High School) and took place in a school complex on the other side of town. There, I was faced with a room full of adults, whose motivation I was not quite sure of. It was an intermediate group, who wanted to improve their English. Most of them were ladies of a certain age, but oddly, one of my pupils in year 11 came along, along with his sister and both parents.

This was a completely different type of teaching, because there was a specified course that you had to follow. It was an extremely dull textbook, consisting of translation and grammar activities, none of which would help in generally improving their English language skills. What was their motivation, I wondered? If they wanted conversational skills that would help them on their holidays, I wasn't providing them. The necessity to follow the allotted course meant that, in my opinion, the lessons were pretty turgid. I did, however, maintain them, on the basis that they were well paid, for a full two years, every Tuesday and Thursday evening. Nobody dropped out and all the participants reliably turned up each session.

There was one particular middle-aged lady who asked me early on if I could give her a lift home, as she lived on my route. Happy to oblige, I agreed to do this. She introduced herself as the mother of one of my pupils in year 5 and, when we got to her house, she stayed in the car and continued nattering to me about her son's progress, because she was worried about it. Unfortunately, she then decided that she was entitled to a lift home after each lesson, and it would have been rude of me to say no. It wasn't long before I realised that what she was concerned about was the possibility of little Hans having to *"sitzenbleiben"*, if he didn't get a good enough grade in English. I had to explain to her that there was no way I could adjust the marks in his favour if he didn't achieve the required standard. It was some time later that the pupil who had brought his family along to the sessions told me that everybody in the class was convinced that I was having an affair with this woman, because we would both climb into my car and disappear at the end of each session. Absolutely nothing could have been further from the truth. After two terms, she was the only one who didn't reappear for the next course.

The rest of us got on just fine, and predictably got into the habit of adjourning to the pub after each session. However, I didn't enjoy teaching adults nearly as much as working with children and teenagers. They were paying for the course, and if they didn't want to do the work, that was their business. Quite often, it was clear that they were mainly there for the social aspect, rather than any motivation for improving their language skills. In a school environment, the teacher is the person in charge and can insist on participation. In this situation however, there was no way you could force anyone to join in if they didn't want to, or were too shy to do, so it wasn't enjoyable for me. I could never understand why they kept coming back.

(iii.) A Little Bit Of Politics

I didn't know it, but taking on those two new year 11 classes was setting me up for a convoluted and extremely difficult future, which I am now going to attempt to explain. All teachers in Germany have the status of a *"Beamte"*. The nearest English equivalent expression for this would be a Civil Servant. It's a very privileged position, because not only are they well paid, but they're also guaranteed a job for life. At the end of my second year at the *"Gymnasium"*, my time with the Centre For British Teachers had come to an end, but I was in a position where I was very happy in my work, my employer was happy with me, and the pupils and their parents wanted me to stay on and see them through to the *"Abitur"*. As my qualifications weren't the required ones for attaining the status of *"Beamte"*, I, along with a couple of other CBT teachers in Bremen, was given a contract as an *"Angestellter"*, which was a temporary arrangement. This was all fine and dandy, and everybody was happy with the outcome.

The problem occurred when I wanted to extend the contract for another year. By that time, I had decided that my destiny was to stay put in Bremen, doing the job I was so much enjoying. The position regarding the teacher shortage, however, had changed completely and now, indeed, there was actually a surplus of teachers. The teaching unions disapproved of people like me occupying positions that they saw as rightly belonging to their members. On top of this, and most importantly, it turned out that there was a law that, if a temporary contract was renewed for a second year, it would qualify as a so-called *"Kettenvertrag"*, which means "chain contract". This would have entitled me to stay on indefinitely. In view of the stance of the unions, the education authority in Bremen decided that none of us English teachers would have our temporary contracts renewed.

Many teachers had taken advantage of the facilities of the Centre For British Teachers and had an enjoyable, lucrative and educationally beneficial time in Germany. Others, however, like me, experienced heartbreaking disappointments and professional setbacks when, having set up firm relationships with colleagues and pupils, we found that our wish to stay on was being denied.

The reaction of most people affected was that this was sad but understandable. Unfortunately, the story here became slightly more complicated, because the contract with the Centre For British Teachers continued, albeit being gradually phased out over several years. This meant in effect that, while established British teachers (some, like me, with exam classes) were finding that their contracts for 1976 to 1977 were not being renewed, new and inexperienced teachers were being recruited in Britain. Not unnaturally, this caused fury among the senior pupils, whose *"Abitur"* (essential for university entrance) was approaching. They found themselves confronted with the prospect of a new teacher taking over their classes and responsible for marking their exams, a mere six months or so before the *"Abitur"*.

In the spring of 1976, the Bremen educational scene was dominated by demonstrations, letters and protests of all kinds by pupils, teachers, parents and, most astonishingly, a concerted front of all the political parties from the CDU (conservative) right through to the various Communist groups. Press, radio and TV covered the situation intensively, focusing at that time particularly on myself, for no other reason than that I happened to have two exam classes. From out of nowhere, I found myself a minor celebrity, as the action escalated. Thousands of pupils, parents and others marched to the town hall in the city square where, in the shadow of the statue of Roland of Bremen, they demanded my reinstatement. A TV crew appeared from Hamburg and filmed a feature on the issue. Every effort failed, however, and at the end of term, no British direct contracts with the Bremen educational ministry were renewed. Why, wondered everybody, particularly enraged parents, was the ministry not prepared to make a goodwill gesture and issue contracts just until exam time, which was all that was being asked? But by then, it had become a matter of principle for the authorities and they weren't going to be seen as bowing to pressure. It was essential that those who had only had one year-long contract should not receive another, because a *"Kettenvertrag"* would legally entitle its holder to extend it ad infinitum. But, confusingly, in less attractive towns such as Bremerhaven, unlimited contracts had been issued to British teachers.

Three different stories resulted from this situation. The first concerned myself. Quite simply, I chickened out, found a job in England and left, although every day, my only wish was to be back in Bremen in my previous position. The second was more interesting. A teacher called Andrew Winter had been fortunate enough to have had two one-year contracts. As the authorities tried not to renew his contract, he stayed on, to fight his case in the courts with the support of the German teachers' union the GWE. He won the initial case, but the ministry appealed. Their appeal was rejected, with the judge making it clear that Mr Winter should be reinstated. The ministry refused to reinstate him and the case went before the *"Bundesamtsgericht"* in Bonn, which ruled for the ministry.

My friend Michael Caldon was in an identical position to me. He stayed on in Germany, initially on unemployment benefit in Berlin and subsequently working for the army there. Determined to return to Bremen and to re-involve himself in the city and school to which he had become so attached, he came back and set about looking for part-time jobs, by putting an ad in the local paper. He little knew that in his old school there was, ironically, an acute shortage of English teachers, and that there was to be a parents' meeting in the presence of Herr Hartmut Hackmack, second in command for recruitment and personnel to the minister, Moritz Thape. Mike discovered that the school had had a parents' meeting the night before on the subject of the teacher shortage, especially the dire situation with English lessons. The parents had got so angry with Hackmack, who was present, that they had demanded something be done immediately. Hackmack replied that there weren't enough English teachers around, whereupon one parent said that, that very Saturday, he'd seen the advert that Mike had put in the local paper, seeking English teaching work. Why couldn't they engage this person?

The Head said, "Okay, if that's what you want, I'll be prepared to engage him." It was at this point in the phone call that Mike said to his Headteacher, "You do realise that's me?" The Head's next step was to go back to Hackmack and say, "I've found this teacher and his qualifications are good, so I'll take him." Hackmack agreed, and then asked what this teacher's name was. Mike Caldon?! The compromise eventually reached was for Mike to accept a limited contract, just teaching his old class for eight hours a week. It seemed a fair solution, but on the Sunday night before Mike re-started teaching, his phone rang and the Head said that a message had come through from Senator Thape that he'd vetoed the appointment. The system had admitted that there was a chronic lack of English teachers in Bremen, but refused to give the schools the English teachers who were there.

Personally, I tried to keep a low profile while all the protests were going on. It was important that I should appear professional, so I declined to get involved. The communist newspapers were all reporting the events, putting their own political slant on them, but I had been assiduous in avoiding allying myself with any particular politics. It would have been very convenient for the authorities if they had been able to pin any communist sympathies on me. I had, by then, moved again, to a slightly larger flat. One day, the landlady, who lived below me, told me when I came home from school that two men had appeared on the doorstep and asked for me. On being told that I was at work, they insisted on coming in (on the pretext that maybe I was in after all and could they knock on my door?). She then heard them moving around in the flat for half an hour, before departing. I am certain that those men were either from the education ministry or the tabloid press, searching for evidence that I had subversive connections. They left empty-handed.

My time in Bremen ended with a farewell party at the school, for which I provided the beer and the music. The pupils had clubbed together and bought me an appropriate leaving gift: a T-shirt inscribed with the message "I like Moritz Thape". This ironic tribute to the education minister showed that I had at least imbued them with an English sense of humour.

(iv.) Love Match

While this political to-and-fro was going on, another *"Wendepunkt"* was happening, that would turn out to be of even greater significance. I had fallen in love with a pupil. It had actually happened on that very first day, as I began the first lesson with the first class I would teach. It would have been quite a thought, that day, to imagine that, nearly fifty years later, we would be doting grandparents.

We all think we know what love is, but I often wonder whether some people go to their graves without ever experiencing it. I had had various girlfriends over the years, and liked them a lot, but I am here to tell you that "love at first sight" does exist. It's hard to explain or characterise, but when I walked into that room, there was a girl sitting three spaces from the front on the right, who made my stomach turn a somersault, a burst of adrenaline explode in my chest and sent my head into a spin. Have you ever felt some doubt when friends or relatives have spectacular weddings but end up in the divorce courts within years? Were they really as in love as they thought they were? Anyway, it hit me like the proverbial sledgehammer, but of course there was never any question of following it up.

I'm not quite sure how Birgit ended up in the Language Branch of the school, because actually, she's better at sciences and is an extremely able mathematician, but there she was, sitting quietly in the default uniform of t-shirt and jeans, mainly looking at the floor and very rarely contributing to the lesson. You could say that she was shy. In the class were some very engaging characters and plenty of enormously bright and very confident students, who were keen to join in at any opportunity. On the face of it, they should have been the ones that I noticed, but they weren't.

As the lessons progressed, it was important for me to involve every pupil in the class in participation. This was vital, in view of the end-of-term oral grade that had to be issued. In yet another permutation of the grading system, two different grades had to be awarded, one for written work and one for spoken work. If there was a crisis caused by indecision as to which eventual overall grade was to be awarded, the oral mark could be used to cancel out deficiencies in the written mark, and vice-versa. If you reached assessment time and had allowed pupils simply not to join in, you would have no evidence on which to base the grading. Therefore, there were occasions where you had to pick on people and insist on them answering the odd question.

Birgit's lack of confidence meant that she seldom put her hand up and would look daggers at me on the occasions when I would require her to participate. There is no evidence that my appearance in the classroom had anything like the same effect on her as she had on me. As far as she was concerned, I was a teacher and, what was more, the grapevine had told her that I was engaged. As far as I was concerned, there was absolutely no question of viewing Birgit in any other way than the other pupils, so I put the raging feelings down to some kind of freak aberration and made sure not to entertain any thoughts of acting upon them. I am actually a pretty moral person with quite high principles, and would doubtless have been very critical of teacher-pupil relationships.

It was about a year before anything happened. Birgit took the tram daily from the school back to her home on the edge of the harbour area, and occasionally I would find myself coincidentally at the same tram stop, where we would indulge in small-talk to pass the time. After a while, I realised that I had unconsciously been timing my walks to the tram stop to coincide with when she would be taking the same route, and our meetings and chats became more frequent. In an unrelated development, she and one of her friends had been invited to join the *"Groschenfêten"*, which took place in various people's homes on a rotating basis.

One winter's evening, a girl in Birgit's class had a birthday party, and I was invited. When the time came to go home, Birgit asked if she could share my umbrella because it was raining heavily, and, as we got close to her home, one of those things happened that in a normal romance would be quite natural. We stopped for a moment and briefly kissed. There was no opportunity for discussion, but I remember quite clearly dancing home in the rain, exactly like Gene Kelly in "Singing In The Rain". I was on a high of euphoria that had completely disappeared by the next morning, when I realised the enormity of what had occurred. One thing was for sure: It was a one-off that could never be repeated.

In the following weeks, there were two more significant get-togethers. One was in my flat, and the other was in the flat of my friend Mike. On both occasions, the other pupils gradually drifted off home, leaving just me and Birgit on our own, pondering what was developing and agreeing that it must not be allowed to happen. We even reached the stage of accepting that we had feelings for each other and that the only solution would be to wait until the end of year 13 before taking it any further. Then, the next thing I knew, Birgit would simply turn up with her bicycle on my doorstep. I would invite her in to discuss how we could not allow this to happen, and then it would happen.

Here I will deal with the moral issue in the best way I can.

From a legal point of view, we were certainly doing nothing wrong. I was young (26) and Birgit was well over the age of consent and absolutely not a childish figure at all. From an educational point of view, however, entering a relationship with a pupil was most definitely wrong, a sackable offence that would have been viewed as a disgrace. But what we had entered into was unstoppable, and from that time on, I lived in permanent terror of appearing in the press in a familiar tale of a seedy old teacher mercilessly exploiting his pupil. Except that the exploitation was entirely mutual. Birgit being a very grown-up person with a strong mind of her own, we were in it together, and therefore it was essential that we were extremely sensible and mature about how we tackled it. In the end, we kept it a secret for round about 18 months, and nobody suspected anything at all. I often think that it is a measure of the strength of our relationship that we succeeded in this, not wanting to take any risks that might jeopardize the future.

One thing that helped enormously was that, before too long, Birgit told her parents about it and they, far from being outraged, immediately expressed their support. They were a very close family and a measure of that closeness was the fact that Birgit felt able to tell them the story, in the confidence that they would support her. The way that it came out is quite a story in itself.

The green Beetle that Herr Illman had lumbered me with had finally reached the end of its road, to the extent that not even the dodgy mechanic with whom Illman was in cahoots could pretend that he could rescue it. I had got by okay using public transport, but now, if Birgit and I wanted to go anywhere together and not be seen, the idea of owning a car became attractive again. As it happened, Birgit's father was in the motor trade, so one day, she explained to him that her English teacher had said that he was looking for a second-hand VW.

In fact, Birgit's father knew of exactly such a car and suggested that we could drive out to a remote second-hand dealership situated in a nearby village. It was a day of such significance to me that I even remember the name of the car salesman, which was Beversen. Helmut, Birgit's father, explained to me later that he had been slightly baffled by his daughter's insistence on coming on this trip with us, since she had never shown much interest in cars previously. When we reached the garage, I knew straight away that this was the car for me. It was a light blue Beetle, not the most basic model, and even had a radio and sunroof. It was precisely what I was looking for and the price was good too, so I bought it on the spot.

Herr Beversen put the cat among the pigeons by observing to Birgit, "It'll be ideal for you and your fiancé to go out in."

"Ha, ha, of course not," guffawed Helmut. "This is her English teacher, not her boyfriend," and we all had a good laugh.

"Don't you believe it," insisted Herr Beversen. "Haven't you seen the way they're looking at each other?"

Helmut was even more surprised when Birgit climbed in beside me in the new car for the trip home, but not even then were his suspicions aroused. However, later that evening, when the family was chatting about what they'd been up to, he said something along the lines that Mr Gray was quite a pleasant guy, and Birgit took the opportunity to tell them what was going on. I think they blinked slightly and were a little bemused but, to their immense credit, they immediately gave it their blessing.

Not knowing much about the education system, they had to be told in no uncertain terms by their daughter that they absolutely must not mention it to anyone. In the following months, I became part of their family and we did lots of socializing, such as hanging out on their allotment, but never, of course, doing anything like going out to pubs. The family was very close, and so it was unavoidable to become involved with extended members of it. I would join in with birthdays and anniversaries and even spent one Christmas with them. There was a particularly eccentric old granny with whom we had to be extra careful because she would be in the habit of indiscreetly blurting things out. This became particularly worrying during the period when I was occasionally appearing on television during the time of the demos, but she managed to keep her mouth shut.

Now that we had the car, we were able to go on outings together by travelling to different places, where it would be unlikely that we'd be spotted. A frequent destination was Oldenburg, about thirty kilometres away, where there were nice restaurants, a theatre, parks and cinemas. Until we reached the Bremen city limits, Birgit would lie on the floor of the car in front of the back seats. This was pretty undignified, but did give us a great laugh, and it certainly worked from the point of view of discretion.

On one occasion, we actually went to Copenhagen to visit Ian, the student who had spent his year abroad in Denmark. We also went on some trips to the island of Wangerooge with some old friends of mine from Kiel uni days. We spent the summer of 1975 together in England, where I worked on my brother-in-law's farm and Birgit helped out with their children. I taught her to drive in my beautiful blue Beetle in the empty stubble fields, something I have never regretted, because Birgit is an extremely good driver and now takes us everywhere.

Meanwhile, the get-togethers with the *"Groschenfête"* gang continued as usual. We probably should have been awarded Oscars for our acting skills, as for near-on eighteen months, nobody noticed a thing, not even when Birgit volunteered to work backstage on the Year 8 class production of "Murder At One". We did do one thing, however, that was stupid and very dangerous. Birgit had a particularly close friend, Petra, and their bond of trust was so strong that Birgit told her about our relationship. That was fine, but what was more problematic was that Petra was going out with a guy called Kurt who was a bit of a druggie, and whom I didn't trust at all. This was all made more complicated by the fact that Kurt had previously been going out with Birgit.

I should have stayed well away from them, but I remember one stupid occasion when I went round to Kurt's flat and we all hung out. For some reason, I remember clearly that we listened to all four sides of Joe Cocker's "Mad Dogs And Englishmen" double album, quite a marathon in itself. We also one day went on a picnic on the banks of the river Weser, and that was when I realised that Kurt was not a reliable character and could easily get us into major trouble if he wanted to.

Ignoring each other in public could sometimes be quite painful. On a particularly awful occasion, I was walking along a corridor at school when I spotted Birgit, who had just come out of a particularly tough oral exam and was sitting in tears on a bench, being comforted by friends. All I could do was walk straight past, not casting her a glance. At around the same time, we both wanted to go to a concert by The Who in Bremen Town Hall. We couldn't be seen together, so went separately and had to pretend hardly to know each other when we passed in the foyer.

We made up for this by going to see the prog-rock band Camel in a nearby town called Cloppenburg, shortly before the end of the third year. One of Birgit's best friends, Elke, decided to come too (I had advertised the show at school) and we managed the whole outing without giving Elke any clue as to our relationship. Camel was an important band to us, because before we got together, I had lent Birgit a copy of their album and pointed out a track called "Lady Fantasy". She didn't get the hint at all. Just as well, since it was a cringingly naff thing to do.

As the year drew towards its end and the political shenanigans surrounding my departure reached new heights, we made sure to be extra-discreet and agreed to meet each other less frequently. If only those guys who were searching my flat had known what they were looking for, they would no doubt have found plenty of evidence, but from beginning to end, the secret was maintained.

The rest is history. We've recently celebrated our fortieth wedding anniversary and welcomed two grandchildren into the family. I hesitate about concepts such as "fate", but this was something that just had to be.

Chapter 4
OLDE ENGLAND

(i.) Home Truths

Finding a new job in England was quite a complicated procedure in those long-before-the-internet days. The only way to advertise teaching vacancies was in the weekly, enormously heavy and thick Times Educational Supplement, a good half of which consisted of "Situations Vacant". I arranged for copies of the paper to be posted to me, and started studying the Jobs section. I was searching for something called a Scale 1 post, effectively a job for a rookie teacher, because my experience in Germany would count for little. It was like going back and starting again, but I didn't have an alternative.

I set aside the May half term of 1976 for a trip to England for some job interviews. I managed to set up three interviews on successive days, in Newport Pagnell, Winchester and Odiham. Newport Pagnell I had only vaguely heard of, but the job looked, on the face of it, to be an appealing one. Winchester I knew because it was quite near to Basingstoke, where the farm was situated, but I had the highest hopes for Odiham, which was a small, pretty town, also in North Hampshire. It seemed likely that it would offer a relatively calm atmosphere in which to start a new life.

Birgit came with me as we flew to Heathrow for a jaunt around the south, which took place by train and bus. The first interview day was extremely stressful, and almost made me want to give up and sign on to the dole, rather than attempt to find a new job. The school in Newport Pagnell was brand-new and hadn't yet been opened, so the interview took place in a teacher's centre in town. The headmaster was the kind of Jack The Lad besuited businessman type that nowadays is common in school hierarchies, but back then was very unusual. The interview was just with him, not with anybody who knew anything about languages, and he seemed to have decided that I was the preferred candidate, as there was no one else to be seen. After a cursory chat, he offered me the job straight away. I was so shocked and taken aback by this that I told him I'd need to think about it. After all, I hadn't even checked out the town and didn't really know anything about what kind of establishment it was going to be.

Jack The Lad seemed to be amazed at my hesitation and started piling on inducements.

"Listen, mate," he said (yes, he called me "mate"), "I'm only allowed to advertise it as a Scale 1 job for now but I can guarantee you will be on Scale 2 within a year."

He seemed to have misjudged me as a character and thought that offering money and status would win me over.

"Thank you, but I'll need a little time to think it over."

"Tell you what, mate, I can guarantee you will be Head of

Department within two years, how about that?"

"Can I think it over, please, just for an hour or so, and tell you then?"

What I hadn't realised at the time was that one of the many anomalies about interviews for teaching jobs in the UK was that you had to make a decision there and then. It was compulsory to advertise all jobs publicly, with no automatic internal appointments being made (although that was often the eventual outcome). If anyone turned down a job offer, it would immediately have to be offered to one of the other candidates. Jack The Lad seem to take it as a personal affront that I was expressing doubts about his wonderful school. I had taken an instant dislike to him and knew in my heart that the job wouldn't be right for me. On the other hand, there was a critical danger that I wouldn't be offered either of the subsequent posts I had applied for, in which case I would have to return to Bremen empty-handed and start all over again.

This being such a quandary, Birgit and I walked over the road to a pub, where I was such a state that I ordered a shot of brandy at lunchtime, something I have never done before or since. Thus fortified, I discussed it with Birgit who, practical as ever, said that I must follow my instincts. I summoned up the courage to return and inform Jack The Lad that I wouldn't be taking the position. He was absolutely furious at my time-wasting, opened the door, gestured to me to leave and didn't even say goodbye.

The following morning saw us arrive in Winchester and take the bus out to a suburb called Harestock. Today's interview was to take place in a comprehensive establishment called the Henry Beaufort School. Arriving early, we had a chance to check out Winchester and realise that it would be a lovely place to live. The school itself was brand new, having been built from scratch in 1971, to service a new estate that had been built on the edge of the city. It had started with just one class, and by the time I got there in 1976, it had reached its full allocation of students. The modern buildings were not particularly attractive, but scattered prettily up the side of quite a steep hill. The atmosphere was friendly in the staff room, as I nervously waited with three other candidates for the interviews to begin.

For some reason, I remember clearly a lady from Scotland, wearing a bright red kilt, who I was sure would be selected for the post, because she was moving from another part of the country, where she was already experienced as a Scale 1 teacher. It was hard for me to assess how I had done in the interview, but to my surprise and pleasure, the headmaster emerged from the post-interview discussion and called me back into his office to offer me the job.

I have often wondered what tipped the scales in my favour, but to provide an understanding of it, I need to describe the school in a bit more detail. The headmaster, Bill Hubert, for whom I felt an instant sense of respect, was a French specialist, who was determined for languages to be a strong point in the school's offering. All pupils were required to take a language from Year 7 (the first year of secondary) onwards, with the option to take up a second language in Year 8. The languages offered were French and German, and I think they felt a desire to strengthen the school's German expertise. They also were interested in my suggestion that I would be able to establish and maintain international links and pen-friendships.

Even so, they were taking a risk in appointing me, because they were well aware that I had no experience in the English school system. I guess my references from Bristol University and Dr Brinkmann must have been strong as well. After a brief conversation with Birgit, I said I would be happy to take the post, rang up the school in Odiham and apologised, but said that I wouldn't be attending for interview. They were almost as irate as Jack The Lad had been, justifiably, because candidates failing to turn up at short notice must be very annoying.

So that was that, and we returned to Bremen to see out the end of the year and prepare to move to England. It wasn't what I wanted, but there was no alternative. When I saw my friend Mike, who decided to stay on and fight, struggling for a couple of years with bits and pieces of freelance work rather than a stable contract, I realised that in one sense, I had done the right thing. In many other senses, I certainly hadn't.

Just before leaving, I was called into the finance department of the city council in Bremen. I dreaded what they might have in store for me, but to my great excitement, they announced that I was entitled to a tax rebate for the last year, and presented me with a couple of thousand Marks in cash. What I didn't realise either was that I would also eventually be entitled to a pension for that period as well, and now I receive a monthly payment of a princely 42 Euros (before tax). It's yet another reminder of how privileged I was to have spent that time at the Gymnasium Waller Ring.

I had accumulated quite a bit of furniture, not all of it stolen from department stores, so began to research how it could be transported. Once again, Herr Lingstädt helped me, by taking me to a friend of his who worked for the international removal firm *"Kühne und Nagel"*. It turned out that it was going to cost thousands of Marks to hire a container, so I persuaded a colleague called Peter Jackson, who was in the same position as me, that we should go halves on hiring a van. He then kindly drove all the way to Winchester, before continuing to his new post in the north of England.

(ii.) Communication Breakdown

A sense of optimism prevailed as I spent the summer again working on the farm, a silly thing to do, as really I should have been getting a break. I tried to suppress the sense of frustration, you know, that feeling when you come back to the bleak UK at the end of a holiday in some beautiful European country? Well, multiply that feeling by three years and add in the underlying emotions. I was aware that I was lucky to have found a nice school in a nice part the UK. I'm pretty sure that Bill Hubert had spotted my socialist beliefs. He had hand-picked his staff from scratch, all of them completely committed to the concept of comprehensive education.

Comprehensive education in the UK is an intriguing concept in a severely class-ridden society. The simple principle is that all students should have the same opportunities. If anybody had wanted to create a school to demonstrate this principle in action at its very best, they could hardly have chosen a better example than Henry Beaufort. In its large catchment area, there were smart houses in leafy suburban streets, as well as two large modern estates of privately owned dwellings, a big council estate and a major army camp in a nearby village. That pretty much covered any social strata in the UK. It suited my egalitarian principles exactly, and it wasn't until much later, when casting around for jobs in other parts of the country, that I realised that such an idyllic example of the comprehensive principle is unlikely to work quite so well in highly-deprived communities. There, middle-class parents typically either move to areas with "better" schools or, like my parents did, bankrupt themselves by paying for private education.

It was with a degree of optimism that I turned up for the first day of the new term. It was a so-called "INSET" day, for staff to get themselves prepared. Within minutes, I was finding myself feeling uncomfortable. The levels of bureaucracy were high, with reminders of all sorts of petty rules that we had to enforce. Prominent among these was the issue of uniform, as detailed by the Senior Mistress, Miss Brandham. This was something I hadn't given any thought to, because in the environment where I had been working, the only important matters had been teaching and learning. Things like which side of the corridor to walk on, gum-chewing and what people were wearing had no significance. In Bremen, girls would often sit and knit throughout the lesson. Why not?

The Senior Mistress went into enormous detail about exactly what was, and was not, permitted in the way of uniform. In a way, the school had brought this confusion upon itself, in an effort to be liberal-minded. Rather than stick to the more conventional blazer / grey trousers / skirts option, they had decided on a "school dress code", based largely on the chosen colour, which was Royal Blue. Miss Brandham explained that it was not permissible for anybody to wear Dark Blue, Light Blue or Navy Blue, only Royal Blue would do. Furthermore, the girls' skirts were allowed to have stripes (of a specific width) but not dots or other patterns. Skirts must be no more than two inches above the knee. As I pictured the staff members on their hands and knees with a ruler, measuring the girls' skirts, I couldn't help but guffaw loudly. A withering look from Miss Brandham showed that she had me marked down as trouble, and indeed she was right. Our relationship would struggle to reach an understanding for the following twenty years. To be fair, she did other aspects of her job very well, so we came to an uneasy truce on the subject of uniform, to which I played half-hearted lip-service.

The Deputy Head, Roy Bone, played a similar rôle to old Bristly-Moustache at Hengrove School, in that he most definitely was a figure to inspire deep respect, nay fear, in potentially difficult pupils. A mere threat to send somebody to see him would guarantee quiet and calm in the classroom. Despite his fearsome reputation, imposing figure and smart pinstripe suit, Roy was a person of great moral stature and calm kindness. I also rubbed along okay with my Head of Department, a lady called Thérèse, who had been there from the start. I think she might have been influential in appointing me, in that she was a French specialist and wanted more strength on the German side. She loved to hold court in the staff room in an atmosphere that was just on the right side of cliquey, with lots of jokes and mickey-taking. We certainly didn't become friends, but were able to work professionally together.

There was one awkward incident, for which I was largely to blame. Thérèse and her husband lived in the countryside near Portsmouth, and invited me and Birgit for a meal at their house. On the day that this was due to take place, I realised that a diary malfunction meant that I was actually supposed to be going to a gig in Southampton. That wouldn't normally have been a legitimate reason for cancelling the invitation, but I was committed to writing a review for the local newspaper. Thérèse was absolutely incandescent with rage and didn't speak to me for weeks afterwards. I have a very vivid memory of her wailing in the staff room in front of all the colleagues, "But we've defrosted four very expensive steaks! What am I going to do with them? Feed them to the dog?" Thérèse ended up as quite a prominent figure in Hampshire politics, eventually rising to become mayor of Winchester.

Did you notice that, in the first chapter of this book, I changed all the names of the staff because of the negative things I had to say about them? By contrast, for this period of my career, I am happy to use all the real names of my colleagues. The reason is that I have nothing bad to say about any of them. I ended up staying at Henry Beaufort for over twenty years. Apart from the extremely rocky start, I had no regrets at all. Populated with intelligent, professional, kind-hearted and gifted staff members, the school was, and remains, an example of comprehensive education at its best. First, however, there was a quite horrible baptism of fire to be endured.

I loaded all my furniture, which had been in storage on the farm, onto a tractor and trailer and drove it over to Winchester. During this process, I suffered several extremely frightening panic attacks, and before I knew it, I was into a full-on nervous breakdown, which hit home during the first couple of weeks of the term. A mixture of anxiety and depression was a potent combination, as I realised that I found myself faced with a concatenation of negative happenings in my life. Firstly, I had been removed from a position of great contentment and relative success, for no fault of my own. Mental crackups, we know, are often caused by things like divorces and bereavements, and this had been a similar occurrence.

On top of that, and arguably even worse, I found myself in intolerable living conditions. In Bremen, I had lived in a comfortable, independent apartment that was easily affordable. In Winchester, all I could find was a tiny, damp, cell-like room in a shared house with people I didn't know and with whom I had absolutely nothing in common. My salary was just over half of what it had been in Germany, and in return, I was asked to do 32 lessons a week, about a third more hours then I had previously been working. Added to that was my realisation that English education was going to involve a huge mass of petty rules and administration (such as twenty minutes of "tutor time" to fill each day before you even started your lessons) plus, of course, the uniform debacle, where I had made myself unpopular immediately.

Additionally, within the first few days, I was verbally attacked by some neighbours, who objected to me parking my beautiful Beetle opposite their driveway, even though there were no parking restrictions on the road. I suspected then, and still do now, that the German number plate and left-hand steering wheel might have induced a racist reaction in them. And finally, I was absolutely exhausted. No wonder I had a bloody nervous breakdown!

I think I managed to get off to a reasonable start as far as teaching was concerned. I followed the age-old rule of being strict at the beginning, with a view to loosening up later. The Year 7 tutor group to which I was assigned was a delight, and we hit it off from the first day, but one huge problem was completely unanticipated. On day one, I found that I had been allocated two classes of English. "Well, we thought you wouldn't mind, as you've been teaching English anyway," said Thérèse glibly.

There is a world of difference between teaching English to foreigners and teaching English to English pupils, following a syllabus with which I was entirely unfamiliar. It was based around "Greek Myths and Legends". The Head of English, Harry Wright, was the most brilliant pedagogue, and no doubt his lessons were exciting and gripping, but I had absolutely no idea what I was supposed to be doing. The only way I was able to teach English was in the form of grammar, but that, as was the trend at the time, was absolutely forbidden. The pupils in those classes wrote endless turgid essays about the activities of Hercules, with poor standards of spelling and punctuation that I was not allowed to correct. To prepare those lessons, on top of my French and German ones, entailed staying up very late at night and planning in minute detail.

After just a few days, I started to have panic attacks in the classroom. It was a feeling of sickness and turmoil in the chest, that made me think I was having some kind of stroke or heart attack. I wasn't able to rationalize these feelings, because, as an adult, I'd never experienced them before. Although it wasn't really that long ago, mental health issues weren't in the general public consciousness as they are nowadays. All I could think of doing was to approach Roy Bone, the Deputy Head, and throw myself on his mercy. It took a lot of courage to do this, because I didn't know him well enough to anticipate what his reaction might be, and he was a stern figure.

In the event, he could not possibly have been kinder, and I owe him a huge debt of gratitude for the practical way in which he approached my problem. He said I needed to consult a doctor and that they would grant me time off school to gather myself together. Then, as now, there was little in the short term that the GP could recommend, other than prescribing drugs. I was first put on a very strong anti-depressant, which I stopped after a few days when Birgit looked it up and discovered that it was potentially highly addictive, and had numerous side-effects.

Birgit, I hear you ask? Yes, she had come with me to England and was working for a family in Winchester as an *"au pair"*. The other pills were standard Valium, in a medium-sized dose. Initially, I decamped back to my sister's house on the farm and wandered round the fields in a daze, feeling that the world had come to an end and that I would be likely to spend the rest of my days in some kind of asylum. Very gradually, however, the Valium started to work, and after a couple of weeks, I was able to go back to school and pick up where I had left off, claiming to the pupils, naturally, that I had had a bad dose of the 'flu.

For the next year or so, I would still have occasional panic attacks in the classroom, and I often wonder whether the pupils noticed that anything was amiss. I certainly remember a few times when I had to go outside into the corridor and take some deep breaths, which surely must have seemed very odd behaviour. Possibly they were so young and innocent that it meant nothing to them; no one ever said anything. In my school days, we'd have been triumphant if we'd hounded a hapless teacher out of the classroom.

(iii.) Day by Day

Life in my little languages bubble was privileged in the extreme. One of the buildings, up some steps at the centre of the school campus, contained something called the Concert Hall, which, as well as being used for performances and productions, served as an overflow gym and a room for assemblies. Next door was the actual gym, plus a small, square space called the Club Room, which had originally been designed for after-school activities. The school having grown so fast, the Club Room was now pressed into service as a classroom, and I was allowed to brand it as a languages area and do all my teaching there. It was my own little kingdom.

Nearly all the teaching I did in my time at Henry Beaufort was based on the audio-visual principles that had been imbued in me by John and Herbie back in Bristol, complete with the reel-to-reel tape recorder and the slide projector. These were huge, heavy pieces of analogue equipment, but they were completely reliable and never let me down once. The German teaching was all done using a course called *"Vorwärts"*, which had been developed in Oxford by the Nuffield Foundation. Anyone who learnt German in that era will be guaranteed to remember the delightful *Hans und Lieselotte*, two youngsters who, with their dog *Lumpi*, their parents and various other characters, lived in the village that was featured in the film strips that accompanied the tapes.

With one pupil at the back turning the film strip and operating the projector, I would play the tape at the front of the glass, pausing frequently for the various elements of audio-visual teaching to happen: listening, choral repetition, individual repetition, followed by O'Neill's trusty substitution drills. Textbooks accompanying the course provided reading and writing practice as well, and the atmosphere in the classroom was always entertaining. There was an intense feeling of uniqueness and privacy because, for the projected filmstrips to be seen, the curtains had to be closed. We were in a little dark cocoon that felt more like an arts centre than a classroom.

The other thing I did to make the classroom feel "languagey" was to completely plaster all the walls with posters that I had brought back with me from Germany. These colourfully featured all manner of entertainments, maps, warnings about smoking and drugs etc. While the caretaker wasn't too pleased about this, especially when he had to try and remove all the Blu-Tak from the walls when it came time to redecorate, it was noticeable that Bill Hubert always chose to bring prospective parents and dignitaries to my room whenever he was doing a school tour. It was just the sort of purposeful but slightly quirky environment that he would have liked to create himself, but couldn't, because of the necessity to present himself as a figure of sober authority.

We could do pretty much whatever we wanted in that room, because language teaching does entail lots of talking. Unfocused chatter was never allowed, but oral drills, singing and conversational practice were a vital part of the learning process. I know for sure that in some schools, language teachers have to hold back on this sort of thing because it is viewed as ill-disciplined if lots of noise is heard emerging from a classroom, but Bill, being a linguist himself, and also dedicated to the audio-visual method, was very relaxed, and indeed positively supportive of our efforts. I rubbed along well enough with Thérèse for a couple of years, until she left to have children and eventually develop her political career, but things got even better with the arrival of her successor, Mike Smith. We had a great deal in common. He was just a couple of years older than me and had previously worked in Wootton-under-Edge, near where I had grown up. He shared all the ideals of the audio-visual teaching method and has remained a lifetime friend.

One technique I used as an aid to motivation was to offer what I called "bribes", for good work or participation. I am aware that giving rewards is a controversial policy, but I made sure that everyone was included and could be part of the fun. Whenever I went to Germany or France, I would collect hundreds of adhesive stickers, which were a big promotional tool at the time. The children adored these, sticking them on their folders and, so the parents told me, on their bedroom walls. Particularly coveted were high-quality decals promoting a chain of German record stores with a friendly alien character called *"Wom'l"*. I still occasionally meet ex-students who tell me how much *"Wom'l"* meant to them. I have thousands of these stickers still in my shed, looking for a good home.

I can only remember one negative feeling from those early years of teaching, and that was the absolutely dreadful French course we were supposed to teach with. Entitled *"En Avant"*, it was the Nuffield equivalent of *"Vorwärts"*, but the quality was terrible and the support offered by the teacher's notes to people like me, whose French could charitably be described as clunky, was incomprehensible. I remember panicked late-night sessions, as I tried to make head or tail of the detailed instructions in the teacher's manual, none of which seemed to make any sense at all. If I could have articulated it then, I would probably have said, "I could do better than this", but at that stage I didn't know how my career was destined to develop.

There was no helpful *"Hausmeister"* around to duplicate materials for us, so we had to do all that ourselves. There was a little recording studio in the main block, where I spent hours on the smelly Banda machine, running off endless worksheets. In what was to perhaps signal my future, I enjoyed this immensely. For my GCSE courses, I created a fifty-page revision booklet, which I also gifted to my colleagues. The Recording Studio was also the venue for both mock and actual oral exams, which entailed days cooped up in the tiny, airless, windowless space as scores of pupils came and went from their twenty-minute grillings.

I can only recall two occasions when I actually got into "trouble" at school. The first was very early on, when I was at my most hesitant and vulnerable. A girl in my tutor group told her parents that I was picking on her. In fact, I had hardly even noticed her and certainly wasn't capable of picking on anyone, but the parents insisted on a meeting with me and Deputy Head Roy Bone. Both the parents were officials in the local scout group and I remember that, for some reason, they turned up in their quasi-military uniforms. They couldn't actually explain in what way I was picking on their daughter, it was just what she had told them. Feeling like I was sitting in some kind of kangaroo court, I remember with shame going to my trouser pocket to access my quarter of a Valium pill, which I kept there for emergencies. Surely they must have seen me slipping it into my mouth? The meeting ended inconclusively and nothing came of it all. Shortly later, the girl decided I was all right after all. I ended up teaching her siblings too, and the parents eventually became friendly and supportive. Years later, they told me that they realised that she probably had just been "going through a phase", but they never apologised for making me feel so bad.

With regard to the medication, I was determined to quit it as soon as possible. I'd always steered clear of any kind of drug, recreational or otherwise, quite unusual for someone who was young in the Sixties. Mental health was not something that was discussed publicly in those days, and I felt terribly ashamed at the thought that I might be hooked on medication, especially after I read up on the subject and discovered how addictive tranquilizers could be. By gradually reducing the dose, I was able to come off the pills, and am glad to say have never needed them since.

In the other "trouble" incident, I felt betrayed by Roy Bone, although I was the one who made the mistake. Once a term, there would be a fire drill. Without warning, a bell would ring out in the middle of a lesson and we would all have to file in silence down to the lower playground, where all the tutor groups would line up and be checked for their presence. I went down the line with the register and was convinced that I had accounted for all the pupils in my group, but in fact I had carelessly not noticed that one boy was absent. This was a little trick played by Roy, which entailed sneaking one child away, to check whether the registers were being carried out properly. Talk about *"mea culpa"*. I felt humiliated, because the whole procedure, including the revelation of the missing child, was carried out in public. It wasn't nice to be made to look foolish, but I damn well made sure never to make the same mistake again.

(iv.) Class Consciousness

After a couple of years, it began to be expected that I should be looking for some kind of promotion. It wasn't what I wanted, because simple classroom teaching was what I was interested in and I knew that I wasn't cut out for extra responsibility and administration. As it stood, there was little opportunity for internal promotion. Both Head of Department Mike Smith and his deputy Rose Brookes were settled in the area with young children, and unlikely to move on. With great kindness and understanding, Bill Hubert arranged for me to be upgraded to a Scale 2 by giving me responsibilities that I was suited to: looking after the language lab, organising the German exchange and being a liaison person for the local press. These were the early days of schools having to consider PR as part of their remit. I was christened "Teacher with Responsibility for German", which suited me fine, because that was exactly where my abilities lay. I took it seriously and worked hard at it.

The language lab would nowadays be regarded as anachronistic and archaic, but back then it was at the cutting edge of technology. In a clear sign of the school's commitment to modern languages, it took up a large room in the centre of the main administrative building. It consisted of thirty-six wooden booths, each with its own reel-to-reel tape recorder for playback and recording. I absolutely loved it in there, sitting on my elevated plinth with my headphones on, feeling like a radio presenter. It was a wonderful facility for the pupils, giving them freedom to experiment in private with their listening and speaking skills, ideal for the more shy among them, but my goodness, it involved a massive amount of work to maintain. I seemed to spend half my life splicing broken spools of tape together.

The only problem with the room was that it was entirely unsuitable for normal teaching and some staff members, who lacked confidence in the technology, found that the partitions between the booths were ideal places for naughty pupils to hide and cause disruption. I would get very upset on the rare occasions that graffiti appeared in the booths. Imprinted on my memory is a dreadful incident that occurred one day, when a boy in the front row suddenly had an epileptic fit in the middle of one of my lessons. It was the first time this had happened to him, so there was no warning and it took a moment to realise what was going on. The poor lad was bashing his head left and right against the wooden partitions, causing bruising and bleeding. In those pre-mobile phone days, all I could do was rush to the school office, where the emergency services were called.

Over the years, I taught thousands of pupils of all abilities. As an illustration of the different kinds of teaching required in a comprehensive school, I can describe two different GCSE classes that particularly stick in my mind. Teaching exam classes required particular concentration, because even back then, schools tended to be measured on their results and each year, people like me, with responsibility for a particular subject, had to be interviewed by the Headmaster and explain and justify the results. One year, I was excited to be allocated the top French class in years 10 and 11. This was quite a privilege, but also a challenge, because of the very high levels of intelligence and motivation of everyone in the class. As a teacher, you really had to be on your game, because a proportion of them was destined to head to university, specialising in languages.

In this particular class were two French native speakers, three super-bright girls who ended up going to Oxbridge, and the extremely gifted son of the school's main French teacher. No pressure, then. Each evening, I swotted up on the next day's topic, and only just managed to keep a couple of steps ahead of them. Indeed, I could see in some of their eyes that they were thinking, "You know what, we actually know more than this guy does". They all ended up getting top grades, which they would have done, with or without my assistance. It was teaching this class that convinced me that I had to do something to improve my French, which led me to apply for a teacher exchange.

At the other end of the scale, you had to spend time with so-called "bottom sets". During the period that covered most of my teaching career, there was a government policy of "languages for all". This meant that it was compulsory for every secondary pupil to take a foreign language up to GCSE level. By no means everybody displayed ability in language learning, and those with the lowest motivation and the least interest would end up in the bottom set. I tended to be allocated more than my fair share of bottom sets, because over the years, I had come to specialise in motivating the least able. I relished the challenge of trying to get the best out of the most uninterested kids, and year after year, would aim at helping them get better GCSE grades than they would normally have expected. I don't know why I enjoyed this type of teaching so much, but it was definitely connected with my strong conviction of inclusivity, that no pupil should be left out and that all of them had the potential to get reasonable results.

The particular class that sticks in my mind was fairly representative of the "bottom set" concept. The majority of the pupils were the salt-of-the-earth, eager-to-please types who just unfortunately didn't have much talent for languages. They were the ones whom I was committed to helping, because, generally, they would sit quietly and do their best. I developed materials to assist them in rote-learning the types of activity they would have to tackle in the exam. But also in the bottom set, there were children with learning and behavioural difficulties, who could easily disrupt the progress of the hard workers. To get the attention of those kids required a high level of energy and a determination to involve every pupil in a non-stop sequence of "entertainment". If you allowed this to slip, it was extremely difficult to claw back the required involvement, and the sufferers would inevitably be the quiet grafters, whom I simply was not willing to abandon.

There were some real characters in that class. One particularly frightening lad would simply ignore everything I said, refuse point-blank to participate, and stare at me throughout with adulterated hatred. Every jolly attempt to chivvy him along would be met by complete contempt and scorn. Whenever there was a written activity and I would collect in the exercise books for marking, each page of his book would be filled with drawings of people attacking each other with knives and chainsaws, blood spurting out of their severed limbs. He ended up getting the lowest possible GCSE grade, but not even he managed to attain the dreaded "ungraded". To do that, I think you had to literally rip up your paper and throw it in the bin. I still think about him today and wonder what became of him.

One of his colleagues in that class was a boy who was generally noted in the school as being troublesome. He would sit in the back row, arms folded and with a supercilious look on his face, saying, "Come on then, entertain me". His mother was a fearsome figure, renowned in the staff room for her tendency to storm into school and berate teachers whom she had perceived to be prejudiced against her son. For me, however, there was something that I really liked about him. He could be extremely funny and, if he was in the right mood, he would participate in the lessons and contribute some good points. He was a keen cyclist, who took part in competitive events. After lessons, he would come to me and talk rather movingly about how his parents were in the process of a very messy divorce. When I asked him what he thought his future held, he had no hesitation. "I'm not going to go to university. I want to go to agricultural college and become a tree surgeon." In the event, he did that very thing and, to this day, I still occasionally employ him to tackle my trees. He's now a contented father and family man.

Do you remember that I warned in Chapter 1 that there has only been one time in my life when I completely lost my temper? It happened in that very class with another type of "bottom set" pupil, namely those who simply couldn't give a shit. There were three girls whose only interest was gossiping about topics such as what they had seen on TV the night before. They sat in a bunch together at the side of the room in the prefabricated overflow hut in which I had to teach (long after the glory days of the Club Room) and completely ignored me, talking non-stop in loud, shrill voices. They didn't even seem to acknowledge their environment, and they certainly displayed zero consideration for the other quiet pupils, who were doing their best to succeed. If I tried to tell them off, they didn't even seem to notice. As an authority figure, I might just as well have not been there. If I tried to separate them, they would either refuse to move or, worse, simply relocated to opposite sides of the room and continued their conversations by shouting across it.

I couldn't bear to witness the sad faces of the conscientious pupils as they observed me being unable to control these losers, and saw their hopes of success being ruined by then. One Friday afternoon, I simply lost it. I can hardly remember any details of what happened, but I know for sure that I ended up bellowing into their faces, probably a bit like the dreadful Spud had done to me at my school, shouting and screaming at them for their selfishness and arrogance. It must have looked appalling - a conscientious adult completely losing his rag and being effectively controlled by a few dumb teenagers. What was worse was that it had absolutely no effect. They didn't even look cowed, and were too lazy even to get their parents to complain. Somehow, we got through to the end of the year and everybody got a grade of some sort, but it's the single event that sticks in my mind, more than any other from my teaching career.

Around a decade later, I visited my dentist for some treatment and was horrified to recognise the face of the receptionist. Yes, it was Sharon, one of the Terrible Trio that I had lambasted in such an uncontrolled way. We pretended not to recognise each other but, when I emerged from the surgery, I heard a voice.

"Mr Gray, can I have a word with you, please?"

"Oh yes, sorry, of course, you want to book another appointment."

"No, I want to apologise."

At this point, there was nothing to be gained from continuing to pretend I didn't know who she was.

"Oh heck, no, I'm the one who should be apologising to you for losing my temper. You do know that was the only time in twenty years that happened?"

"Well, I've been waiting for an opportunity to apologise for the way we behaved. We often meet up and look back on how badly we treated you and how selfish we were in that class. All I can say is that it was just terrible teenage behaviour and that we all feel deeply ashamed."

Time certainly heals. I encountered Sharon on many more visits to the dentist and we always had positive and pleasant chats. I was pleased that she had actually managed to "make something of herself".

(v.) Un, deux, Troyes

Teaching the class of high-flyers, and only just about getting away with it, made me realise that I urgently needed to do something about improving the quality of my French, so I applied to the Bureau for Educational Visits and Exchanges to spend a period of time teaching in France. As we had a two-year-old daughter and no idea how such an exchange would work out, I opted for a single term rather than a whole year, with the option of an extension. The system was remarkably similar to the one that had taken me to Germany in 1973: You simply had to apply, and then go wherever you were sent.

Before long, I received a letter saying that I would be posted to the Collège Beurnonville in Troyes, south-east of Paris. Prior to departure, there was a brief training course that took place at Brunel University in Uxbridge, where we were given some tips for survival in a foreign school. Something that failed to fill me with optimism was an awful scenario, where they rolled out a poor Spanish teacher who was doing an exchange and had landed in what was clearly an extremely rough school in outer London. When her turn came to stand up in the lecture hall and tell us about her experience, she burst into tears, telling us how cruel, racist and generally vile the English pupils were being to her, and that she couldn't wait to go home. This wasn't quite the message she was supposed to be conveying, and I hoped that Troyes would turn out to be a better environment.

The similarities with Bremen continued when we packed up our tiny Mini Metro and travelled, with our little daughter, to Troyes, which we had scarcely even heard of. That was our loss, as Troyes turned out to be an idyllic, unspoilt, half-timbered mediaeval city. The arrangement was that we would live in the apartment of the teacher who was doing a swap with me, a lady called Françoise. She was an ideal exchange partner, because her motivations were identical to mine: simply to improve her English. Françoise, in turn, would live in our house near Winchester.

Apart from the fact that we almost had a fatal crash on the Paris *"Périphérique"* and arrived in Troyes with the exhaust pipe hanging off and had to spend the first day getting it repaired, I was feeling optimistic, if very nervous. I had formulated a plan to do the same as I had in Bremen, which was tell the pupils that I couldn't speak French and conduct all the lessons entirely in English. This time I wouldn't need to pretend. The plan didn't work out, though, because it transpired that I was to be given far more in the way of responsibility than I had anticipated.

On a continuing theme of similarity to Bremen, the school was in an identically gloomy building, situated right in the centre of the city. It again had the air of an extremely intimidating barracks or prison, a sparse, stone edifice with tiny windows and no green space around it at all. By now, I knew that appearances could definitely be deceptive and, once again, it turned out to be a friendly, welcoming and pleasant institution in which to work.

Day One brought a bit of a shock. I wasn't just to be a guest teacher, I had to take on the full-scale rôle of *"Professeur Principal"*, which was the equivalent of a form tutor. My job was to initiate the beginners' class I was allocated into all the customs and conventions of the school. I was given a piece of paper where all this information was listed, and had just one evening to get my head around it and find the words to convey it in French to the assembled eleven-year olds. Just to give a flavour of some of it, here is a brief (translated) extract:

- Do the register and write down who is present in pencil. Do not cross out any names, just write absent.
- For ambiguous Christian names, establish whether it's a boy or a girl.
- Compile a list of *demi-pensionnaires* (people eating lunch at school).
- Send the register to the school office.
- Dictate the timetable. Convey the names of the teachers.
- Get students to write the timetables for weeks A and B in their notebooks.
- Point out the locations of the classrooms and in particular, the library and gymnasium.
- Tell the pupils to bring ten envelopes with stamps to the value of 2 Francs 20 attached to the envelope, format 15.5 by 11cm.
- Collect 15 francs from each pupil for the school fund.
- Collect 20 Francs from each pupil for science outings.
- Tell pupils with bikes that they must bring a lock and emphasize the dangers of cycling in traffic.
- Remind them that motor scooters are not allowed to be ridden in the playground.

… and that was only half of the first page.

To attempt to convey all of this in English to a bunch of

young children who hadn't even started to learn the language would have been futile, so my French skills were put to quite a challenging test from day one. The kind pupils, who were probably just as intimidated as I was to be entering a new environment, dutifully wrote it all down and carried out the instructions to the letter.

What I also had in my favour was the pupils' attitude, which was identical to that of the German pupils. I was treated as an honoured guest, an exotic creature who was to be admired and revered. Apparently, the other beginners' classes were extremely jealous that they, too, hadn't been given an English gentleman to teach them.

The timetable was less intense than my English one, but slightly more so than the German one had been. I was allocated six different classes at different levels, and soon was able to relax. It was a *"Collège"*, a state secondary school covering pupils of all abilities up to the age of 16, when they would transfer to the local *"Lycée"*, or sixth form college. All the children came from the local urban area and, to my pleasure, it was my first experience of a multicultural audience, with a good number of Arab students and also quite a few from Portugal.

I was supposed to be working with a specific course book, but the delightful head of department, Colette, told me that she felt it was more important for the pupils to take advantage of being taught by a native speaker. The other teachers didn't really like the course book anyway, so I used the freedom to make my own materials and adapt existing ones. I had brought with me some things which I knew would act as motivators, and plastered the classroom with English posters. I also had a large bag of "bribes", which went down a storm.

The school day was very long, starting at 8 a.m. and not finishing until 5. There was also school on Saturdays, but that was compensated for by having Wednesdays off. This was brilliant, because Troyes was situated just by the *"Forêt d'Orient"* National Park, and we were able to drive out and spend each Wednesday by one of the many lakes there. Another thing that made the days easier was the enormously long 90-minute lunch break, during which the pupils were served up a three-course gourmet French meal, which I also tucked into with alacrity, although deemed it wise to avoid the wine that was also on offer (to staff only). As a souvenir, I brought home the menu for the week of 18 November, 1985. I can't resist reproducing it here:

- *Lundi:* Crudités – saucisses grillées – Lentilles au lard
- *Mardi:* Sardines/beurre – Boulette sauce tomate – Épinards – Kiri-fruit
- *Jeudi:* Crudités – Beefstaek (sic) – Pommes frites – Pâtisserie
- *Vendredi:* Salade verte - Omelette nature – Raviolis gratins - Yaourt/fruit
- *Samedi:* Mortadelle – Poulet rôti – Petits pois – Fromage/fruit

You simply couldn't get any more French, could you?

There were no playground duties because of the system of *"surveillants"* (nicknamed *"pions"*), who were local university students who were paid to look after the pupils outside lesson times. In England, I used to hate days when there was no respite between lessons because of playground duties and lunchtime supervision. It was exhausting. In France, I was considered very odd, because I brought in a flask of tea to consume at break, but it emphasised my English credentials of eccentricity.

We hadn't been aware that Troyes was the capital of the Champagne region of France. Several of the pupils were the children of vineyard owners and when the time came, after just a week, for the first parents' evening, I was amazed and gratified to find that several of them turned up with bottles of champagne as gifts. Not only that, various families invited us out to their houses for meals. This meant that, by the time we returned at Christmas time, I had put on quite a few pounds and had experienced quite a few examples of the kind of vicious hangover that can only come from drinking large amounts of champagne, which in this region was dished out like lemonade.

As we had had such a fabulous time, and as I could already tell that my French was improving rapidly, I tried to cash in the option of extending my stay for another couple of terms. When I did a mid-term course in Paris, I discovered that many of the other English teachers scattered around France were equally enamoured, and had decided to do the same. Sadly, there was a problem in my case. Back in Winchester, poor Françoise was having a rotten time. It was at the height of the popularity of the TV series "'Allo 'Allo", and Françoise had a very strong French accent. Well, I certainly had a very strong English accent, but the French pupils, far from taking the piss out of it, seemed to find it charming and were incredibly warm and kind towards me. Not so the nasty little oiks in England, who were being so beastly to Françoise that she made it clear that no way was she going to stay on a moment longer than she absolutely had to. For me, the experience had been tiring but incredibly positive. My French was vastly improved and it served me in very good stead for my future career. We are still in touch with some colleagues in Troyes and visit as often as we can.

(vi.) Promo

After a few more years, it was mentioned on a few occasions by senior management that I really ought to be thinking about applying for a Head of Department job somewhere. This wasn't because they wanted to get rid of me, just that they were kind and professional senior managers, keeping an eye on the progress of their staff. The trouble was, that such an undertaking would entail major personal upheaval, and possibly moving to another part of the country. Because we now had young children, we had no desire to move away. Birgit was settled in a great job as a community midwife based at the local hospital and Winchester was a brilliant place to live. Another consideration was that any pay rise involved would be minimal and not come close to covering the costs of moving house.

On one occasion, a Head of Department post cropped up in one of the two other local secondary schools. I knew that this school had quite a different ethos from Henry Beaufort and that I would be unlikely to fit in. My performance in the interview was mediocre at best, because in my heart, I definitely didn't want the job. In any event, it went to an internal candidate in a stitch-up job. Far from being disappointed or resentful, I was actually quite relieved to find myself back in the classroom, where I belonged. In the de-brief after the interview, the local languages advisor, a lady who treated me with disdain (the feeling was mutual) told me that I would have a better chance if I got a haircut and dressed properly. If those were their educational priorities, I wanted no part of it.

Another possibility might have been to aspire to such an advisory post myself, but my experiences with advisors on various training courses I undertook led me to feel very negatively towards them. They tended to be grey people in grey suits, and my feeling was that they had got themselves promoted in order to get out of the classroom, where I could only assume they had had a hard time, considering the terminal dullness of the courses they ran. In professional terms, I was the exact opposite, in that fooling around in the classroom was my natural environment, and that was where I wanted to stay.

Idiotically, I did apply for various other Head of Department jobs over the years. This gave me a deep appreciation of how lucky I was to be in the environment I found myself in at Henry Beaufort. I presented myself at a secondary school in Hamble, a pretty village near Southampton. I thought that would potentially be an attractive prospect, but on interview day, the school turned out to be very rough indeed. I have a memory of one of the staff, an ex-naval officer, bizarrely still dressed in some kind of naval uniform, taking me aside at break-time and whispering to me, "This place is a shithole, don't touch it with a barge pole". I took his advice and withdrew my application before the interview.

A more attractive proposition was a modern school in nearby Romsey, which had a reputation for being strong in languages. It was very well-equipped and the temptation was strong to give it my best shot, although I was hesitant, because it would have involved either a house move or a forty-minute commute. It was daunting, because the HoD I would have replaced was a very dynamic teacher, who had been promoted to an advisory position. As it happened, the post went to an internal candidate anyway, and I drove home with a strong sense of relief. The expression "Be careful what you wish for" seemed apt.

Among other schools I looked at was a comprehensive in the West Country, where the head teacher was the mother of one of my best friends. I think we would have considered the possibility of a family move to a different area, because we had fallen in love with Dorset, but the day was an absolute shocker. Discipline in the school was non-existent. Part of the procedure was for us candidates to spend time in classrooms, guesting in lessons which were taking place. I was shocked and almost frightened by the level of chaos and anarchy. There was absolutely no learning going on whatsoever, with the children running riot around the classroom. This was them on their best behaviour to welcome honoured guests! I'd never seen anything like it, and once again withdrew my application before being interviewed. It was slightly embarrassing for my friend's mother, but I lied to her and said we didn't think we could face moving the family all that way for a few more pounds a month.

One alternative to horrors such as that might have been to consider applying for jobs in the "private sector", but once again, I knew it would be impossible for me to fit in there. My own school days had turned me into an implacable opponent of elitist education systems and I was, and remain, in favour of the abolition of private schools, so throwing in my lot with them would have been hypocritical in the extreme. When we moved to England, Birgit initially worked as an *au pair* in the family of a teacher at the expensive public school Winchester College. I'll never forget her reaction when they kindly took her on a visit to the school dormitories. "My god," she cried, "it's like a cross between a prison and a youth hostel. You're not telling me people actually PAY for this?"

When our children were young, our social circle was widened by attending play-schools, where we met some wealthy and entitled people, whose paths we normally wouldn't have crossed. Coming from the more egalitarian German society, Birgit hadn't previously come across the concept of "posh", and even I was surprised by the complacent attitudes that abounded. One family sent all their children to Winchester College as boarders, despite living less than a quarter of a mile away. What's the point of having children, we would ponder, if all you want to do is get rid of them?

I remember one occasion when our daughter was having some issues at primary school and we were discussing how to approach the problem and solve it. "Why don't you just send her to private school?" asked one of these entitled ladies, clearly without any awareness that not everyone has the thousands of spare pounds available to spend in this way. I didn't know where to start in response, so just kept my mouth shut.

It has been interesting to observe the progress of the offspring of the various families we met at that time, who sent their children to private schools. For a start, their friendships with our children came to an end, because they had been transferred into a different, elite environment. Without exception, they progressed to the "best" universities, now occupy well-paid jobs in areas such as finance, live in large opulent houses and, of course, send their children to private schools. That's what I call a broken society.

(vii.) Fair Exchange

A few words are now needed to justify my assertion that Henry Beaufort School was a fine educational establishment. The maths department had a fearsome reputation for discipline, and their regimented teaching style was in stark contrast to the rather more relaxed approach of the languages department. Nevertheless, they were outstanding maths teachers, who filled the kids with respect and a solid work ethic, so their results were always excellent. On the English teaching side, there was a happy mixture of experienced, wise old owls and enthusiastic, highly creative young beginners. The drama department was run by an utterly inspirational teacher called Noel Thorpe-Tracey, who had the admiration of everyone he came into contact with.

There was a very businesslike department covering practical subjects and art. Bill Hubert was determined that all boys should learn to cook and that all girls should take part in activities such as woodwork and metalwork, previously seen by some as a male domain. In this, Bill was typically well ahead of his time. The music department catered both for classical musicians in the Hampshire County Youth Orchestra, which was based there, and more modern music styles, performed on their large selection of electronic instruments. What I had known as geography, history and social studies were lumped together in the Humanities department, which contained the most politically radical staff. I got on tremendously with David Taylor, the Head of Humanities, who was fully committed to local social history projects, focusing on the surrounding villages and encouraging the children to do original research. It was all a far cry from those dreaded kings and queens of my youth.

Talking about politics, every staff member was part of a Trades Union. The two most prominent ones were the NUT and the NAS/UWT. During my years there, we took part in several natonal strikes over a variety of issues, mainly matters of workload and poor pay. Bill Hubert's heart was completely with his staff. Although he couldn't come out and publicly support strike action, he always made arrangements for it to take place unhindered, while the school continued to function.

Sport worked well at the school. My little classroom was right in the centre of the hive of sporting activity presided over by a succession of highly skilled PE teachers, one of whom, Helen Rollason, went to go on to become a National Treasure in her subsequent media career. Boys' sport, too, was different from the military-style regimented approach I had had to suffer in my youth.

The only department with which I had the occasional minor niggle was science, which was run by a strutting, rather arrogant character, who very much disapproved of me walking around with my leather jacket, long hair and, particularly during the punk era, badges of various kinds attached to my lapel. On one occasion, he stormed into a lunchtime music session where I was playing some loud music and accused me of being a "selfish bastard".

Each teacher had to be committed to undertaking certain extra-curricular activities. As I was unable to offer anything in the way of sport, I invented a concept which proved extremely popular and lasted for many years: a weekly lunchtime session called Rock Club. This took place in the music block. All that happened was that students would bring in their albums and singles and we would loaf around and listen to them for an hour or so. There was occasional controversy, especially with the arrival of Punk in 1977, when a battle royal took place between punk rock and the "Progressive" music old guard, which Punk won.

Unsurprisingly, the Punks caused all sorts of problems with the pro-uniform brigade, as they did absolutely everything they could to bend the rules. There were two punk rock girls in my tutor group who delighted in wearing their hair in spiky, multicoloured styles and holding meetings advocating anti-vivisection and animal rights. I thought all this was super-cool and supported them and their enthusiasm. Miss Brandham, of course, was mortified but, to her credit, never made a big issue out of it.

As the languages department was so committed to international understanding, foreign exchanges and trips were a very important part of the programme. Foremost among the activities was the annual trip to Luxembourg, which every ex-pupil I ever meet cites as the highlight of their school career. The first time I took part in one of these sorties, the whole thing took place by ferry and train. You can only imagine the potential for chaos and disaster as a few staff and sixty twelve-year-old pupils travelled half-way across Europe to stay in a youth hostel in the Grand Duchy.

Of the hundreds of crazy memories, one that stands out was future famous actor Rhashan Stone sitting on his rucksack at Waterloo Station and crushing several cartons of yoghurt that his parents had helpfully placed at the top. Every stitch of his clothing was impregnated with smelly, rapidly mouldering dairy product. In Luxembourg, I personally had to spend an entire day in a dental hospital after one of the female pupils had her two top front teeth knocked out by a hairbrush falling on her from the top bunk in the dormitory.

On the return journey, a young lad caught his finger in the lavatory door on the train. In those pre-mobile phone days, the only way we could sound the alarm was to write a note requesting that an ambulance should meet us at Brussels station, wrap it up in a roll of toilet paper and hurl it out of the train window as we passed through a remote station. Remarkably, this worked and the finger was saved.

In subsequent years, the trip took place by coach, which made such travel mayhem less likely, but still there were plenty of mad tales. At one stage, we found ourselves in a zoo near Luxembourg City, which was so run-down that the elk and deer were being fed to the wolves for breakfast.

One important element of these trips was to give pupils the opportunity to interact with the locals and to practise their language skills. One particular memory is of a young boy called Sean, who was not exactly gifted in the languages department, but full of enthusiasm. After an hour walking around Bernkastel with his clipboard and questionnaire, he returned to announce proudly to us teachers, "Mr Gray, Mr Smith! Guess what? I asked twenty-seven people the way to the town hall and all of them knew the answer!"

School pupil-to-pupil exchanges were a different type of thing, involving enormously complicated preparations and huge levels of responsibility. It was all worthwhile, because in the end, just as happened to me in my teens, many of the kids forged lifelong friendships and love of other European countries. The French exchange was with a school in a beautiful hilltop town in Normandy called Avranches. This was organised by the main French teacher, Rose Brookes, but I went along as a support teacher, taking Birgit and the children and camping on the beach at Jullouville.

The German exchange was entirely my responsibility. For the first few years, we hooked up with a school in Cloppenburg, a nice but dull north German town, which I had got through my contacts in Bremen. The journey there was invariably convoluted and incident-ridden, including an overnight ferry to the Hook of Holland, where we teachers had to stay up all night to stop our teenage girls being ravaged by the drunken, aggressive English squaddies heading to their German barracks. One year, the train split into two in the middle of traversing Holland, and we discovered that half our pupils were in the process of being whisked off to far-away Scandinavia. By the grace of God, both trains stopped briefly in Osnabrück and we were able to rescue them. That would have been a hard one to explain to Bill Hubert at a subsequent de-brief.

As all this was far too stressful, I started a new and more satisfactory exchange with a school in Hamburg, to where we could fly, avoiding most life-threatening incidents. This wasn't a given, however. On one occasion, a boy had an epileptic fit (yes, another one, although it was a different boy) on a jaunt with his exchange partner to the city centre, knocking himself unconscious on the floor of McDonald's. I was charged, for the return journey, with the job of administering a suppository if he showed signs of another attack. There was a strong sense of relief as I safely delivered him back to his parents.

The enthusiastic German host families would invite our pupils to undertake all sorts of dangerous activities such as windsurfing, horse riding and go-karting. As interaction with the families was the major purpose of the activity, I could hardly forbid those things, but I don't think our insurance policy would have been up to covering any accidents.

My favourite tale from the exchange era came from Caroline, a particularly gifted pupil, who in fact went on to study German at university. She had a great week travelling around the Hamburg area with her exchange partner and chums. Public transport in Germany runs on a system whereby you purchase either a monthly pass or a ticket in advance. No money changes hands while travelling. I only realised what she had inadvertently been up to when she handed in the essay that I always demanded after an exchange, reflecting on the pupils' experiences. Caroline enthused, "I was particularly impressed by the German transport system. Not only are the trams and buses clean, fast and efficient, they are also entirely free!"

It didn't do to think too much about it, but of course I did exactly that, and eventually the stress of the responsibility became too much and I stopped organising exchanges.

In view of how my life was going to pan out, I now consider that it was fate that decreed my failure to become a Head of Department. I am sure that I would have suffered another nervous breakdown. Around the period when I was making those applications, no fewer than three of my colleagues at school retired "on grounds of ill health", and I know for a fact that it was the stress of Head of Department responsibilities that was the cause. As I meandered on with my day-to-day Scale 2 teaching, I occasionally felt some slight resentment, because they all got payoffs and pensions, but I was saddened to watch them going through hell on earth, battling anxiety and depression. I had unwittingly dodged a bullet, but in my heart, I knew that I couldn't bear the thought of ending up as that farty old teacher that everybody takes the piss out of because he's gradually losing the plot. It was either that or end up like those colleagues, and neither held much appeal. There had to be some kind of way out, but what would that be?

Chapter 5
AUTHOR, AUTHOR

(i.) Getting booked

Dragon's Den entrepreneurs often talk about an "exit strategy". I should have had such a strategy for getting out of teaching. Teaching is a young person's game and, for the sake of both pupils and the sanity of their instructors, teachers really shouldn't carry on beyond the age of about 50. That was my belief anyway. My fruitless attempts at getting new jobs in teaching had convinced me that that was the wrong route. I did occasionally half-heartedly scan the Guardian's media job section once a week, and I actually did apply for a couple of publishing jobs, but withdrew on discovering that their salaries were considerably lower than even that of a Scale 2 teacher, and that the jobs would have entailed commuting to London. Little did I know that the exit strategy was staring me in the face, but that it would only be achieved with a great deal of serendipity, pure fluke, and the help of some very kind and supportive colleagues.

Back in 1975, in Bremen, I had been approached by my much-revered Deputy Head, Dr Hans Brinkmann. I already knew that he was quite a well-known author of English language teaching books. He had had one particularly successful project called "How To Avoid Mistakes", which was used widely throughout German secondary schools. The principle of this was simple: there are certain mistakes that learners of another language are particularly prone to make, on the basis of their mother tongue. There are thousands of examples of this, but simple ones are the way Germans tend to say "heppy" instead of "happy" or use a different word order ("We go often to the cinema").

Dr Brinkmann's idea was that, if you could focus in closely on these typical errors and eliminate them, you were well on the road to language perfection. When he approached me for help, he had no idea of my background in Kiel, where I had been researching exactly this in my "interference" thesis. Dr Brinkmann had been commissioned to write a series of workbooks to accompany his text book. These workbooks were to be called "Practise Avoiding Mistakes", but he was worried that his English was rusty. He thought my up-to-date knowledge of current English would help make the workbooks more colloquial, and he was right.

I set to work with enthusiasm, creating exercises and activities based on the themes focused on by Dr Brinkmann (we never reached first name terms, as that is a long and convoluted procedure in Germany). Before long, the workbooks came out and started to be used in German schools. It did cross my mind that perhaps I should have been paid for this work, but Dr Brinkmann reassured me by simply saying, "Don't worry, I'll make it worth your while." Thus, it was quite a disappointment when he came into school one day with a bottle of whisky and gave it to me by way of a thank-you. A lot of people assume that my Scottish heritage indicates that I ought to love whisky. In fact, I can't stand it, and ended up giving the bottle away.

I should never have doubted him, though, because it turned out he had quite another way of rewarding me in mind. This took the form of introducing me to his employer, a large educational book publisher called Diesterweg, based in Frankfurt. Before long, I was approached by the editor-in-chief of the English department, a lady called Doris Jacoby, who asked if I'd be interested in writing some workbooks, for use in the upper years of German grammar schools. These were compilations of texts, accompanied by comprehension questions and discussion suggestions.

During the first year or so of feeling all-at-sea in Winchester, this was a hobby that helped keep me on an even keel. Bearing in mind the popularity of *"diskutieren"* in English lessons in Germany, I set about sourcing and adapting texts on matters that provoked a range of opinions and a level of controversy. Among the booklets that I created were one on the "British Press", one on the "Nuclear Debate" that was raging at the time, and one called "Man Against Nature", about environmental concerns, which were in their infancy. Without really trying, I had entered the world of educational publishing, and I found it both stimulating and rewarding.

During this period, Doris Jacoby found herself at the centre of a minor controversy herself. Paul Theroux, father of Louis, wrote an excoriating article in The Times, in which he lambasted the publisher Diesterweg for appropriating his work. An obscure German law made it perfectly legal to take other people's copyright material and use it without payment, so long as it didn't exceed a certain length and was specifically intended for educational purposes. When Paul Theroux approached Diesterweg and asked them to either desist or pay him, Doris cited this law in her response. Therefore, nowadays, whenever I see Louis Theroux on TV, I feel a slight twinge of guilt that my publisher might have marginally diminished his inheritance. I hasten to add that I was not the writer who stole his text.

Now established as a writer for Diesterweg, I was again asked to help Hans Brinkmann, because they wanted to cash in on the success of "How To Avoid Mistakes" by producing a version for younger pupils, aged around twelve to fifteen, from vocational as well as grammar schools. This was to be called simply "Avoiding Mistakes", and was to combine the text book and the practice book into one volume. This time, I would be co-author and on a percentage of the royalties, so Hans Brinkmann really had come good on his promise. I worked on the project for a good few months and when it was published, it became an immediate success. This is hard to fathom now when you look at it, because all it is really is a series of densely packed, small-print pages full of traditional exercises, but it suited the formal teaching approach prevalent in German schools.

Astonishingly, "Avoiding Mistakes" still sells today, over forty years since it was first published. It was given a boost in 2014 when Diesterweg asked me to update it in line with modern colloquialisms. Dear Dr Brinkmann had died a few years previously. Brinkmann's daughter Marita arranged for me to do the updating, and that exercise was an eye-opener in itself, as it made clear just how not only language but social attitudes had changed. One example that made me gasp was the use of the word "negro". I can clearly remember how important it was to use this word, because back then to call someone "black" would have been deeply offensive. I have always been perfectly happy with the idea that language is constantly changing, and I'm very much in favour of careful choice of words in order not to discriminate or offend anyone, so I was happy to set this right in the reprint. Among many other anomalies were old-fashioned names, a complete lack of any kind of multiculturalism and not a single reference to computers, mobile phones, the internet or modern technology in general. All that has now safely been updated.

One of the French teachers at Henry Beaufort school was a lady called Gillian Taylor, who was just setting out on a career path that was lead her to become a successful and renowned author of language teaching books. For Longman, a major UK educational publisher, she had written a French practice book called *"Tu Parles Français"*, which had sold in very high numbers. I loved this book, because it was a very clearly-constructed, highly-illustrated classroom aid, packed with useful and accessible material for the GCSE exam. Among several innovative concepts that subsequently got taken up and used by mainstream language courses were grids, which provided ready-made adaptable language that pupils manipulated in quite a similar way to the Substitution Drills of yore. At the simplest level, it could be something like this:

If you are going shopping, there are some simple sentence structures that you're likely to use, such as "Do you have …?", "Have you got any …?", "What kind of … do you have?", "How much is …?", and so on. Or, if you are using public transport, it could be phrases such as "Where is …?", "How do I get to …?", "What time does the … leave?", "How much is the ticket?" etc. This type of approach was ideally suited to the teaching method of the time. It had moved on from the "audio-visual" method and become known as "transactional language".

Two very important things had happened in the evolution of language teaching in the UK. The first was the almost entire removal of grammar from the syllabus, and the second was the idea of promoting learning a language so that you could actually use it. I was strongly committed to this latter approach, especially because, in the early nineties, the policy of "Languages For All" had been introduced, meaning that it was compulsory for all secondary pupils to take a language at GCSE level. It was also increasingly likely that young people would be going abroad with their parents on holiday. Their parents, like me, had been taught in an old-fashioned grammar-based manner, which meant that they were unlikely either to be able to speak or understand with any confidence. Personally, I was always in favour of a more middle-of-the-road approach, which would include elements of grammar alongside the transactional language.

Because of the success of *"Tu Parles Français"*, Longman were looking to diversify the concept into other languages.

Gill Taylor didn't speak German but, knowing that I had publishing experience, asked if I would like to write the German version, whose title was to be "*Sag Mal*". Of course I jumped at the opportunity and, even though I was on quite a small percentage, I was thrilled to see it selling in good numbers over a period of years, and running to several reprints and a couple of revised versions. I used it every single day in the classroom and was thankful for its help in attaining good GCSE results for many pupils who otherwise might not have succeeded. In saying this, I am not praising myself, rather paying tribute to the imagination and skill of Gill Taylor.

Still hanging on the shirt-tails of others, another project with Gill was just around the corner. She had the idea of compiling a puzzle book, practising foreign language vocabulary, for the publisher Hodder and Stoughton. Once again, she was stumped when a German version was mooted, and I jumped to the rescue. This time I was on a higher percentage rate because I contributed more creative input, spending a few weeks inventing crosswords, word-searches, mazes and other such brain-teasers. The resulting book, imaginatively entitled "German Vocabulary Through Puzzles" was also a good seller and extremely useful in my own lessons. If you were feeling a bit tired or lazy, you could hand out photocopies of the puzzles and get the pupils to occupy themselves.

I guess this was the period of my life when I was working hardest, because I was a bit of a sucker for punishment. Not only was I teaching a full timetable, I was also now writing text books, doing a weekly radio show for the BBC, writing Live reviews for music papers, promoting live gigs and also, just as a sideline, managing a rock band. This entailed travelling around the country to gigs and often not getting home till the middle of the night. Somehow, I avoided a second nervous breakdown, and I think the reason for that was simply that, although all the activities were very tiring and time-consuming, they were also, in different ways, all enjoyable and fulfilling.

(ii.) On the cards

Round about 1989, yet another *"Wendepunkt"* was set to transform my life. Central to the teaching techniques of the time, because of their prevalence in the reading element of the GCSE exam, was the concept of "authentic materials". This meant that pupils were expected to read for a purpose, and that anything they read was supposed to fit into the category of "realia", by which was meant actual genuine items in the target language, rather than ones dreamed up by text book writers or examiners. Thus, for example, in exam papers and practice materials, there was a prevalence of things such as maps, train timetables, menus, extracts from tourist brochures, advertisements and other things that a traveller would encounter and have to interpret while abroad. Again, I enthusiastically supported this approach, because it seemed to be so sensible and practical, and certainly a lot more helpful than swotting up on grammatical terminology.

For many years, on the annual school trips, I had been collecting large amounts of "authentic materials" and bringing them back to use in school. So, for example, if the topic was finding the way round a town, I would distribute a genuine tourist map of Bremen to every pupil. Instead of looking at a map reproduced in a book, or a photocopied version, everyone in the class would have their own map, thus making the activity more realistic. Or, if the topic was ordering a meal in a restaurant, everyone would have their own menu. This entailed collecting enormous amounts of paper and lugging it all back home. One year, Mike Smith and I emerged from a tourist office in Luxembourg with our rucksacks so laden down with material, that we were walking along leaning backwards at an angle of 45 degrees.

The light-bulb moment occurred to me in a most unlikely place. On a Christmas visit to Germany, Birgit and I were on a ferry heading for the North Sea island of Wangerooge, where we planned to spend a few days, having left the children with the grandparents. Birgit suffers extremely badly from seasickness, and it was a very stormy day, so she huddled in a corner on her own. Meanwhile, in search of something to read, I picked up a copy of a listings magazine that was lying on a table in the snack bar. As I leafed through it, it struck me that it was crammed with exactly the kind of materials the English pupils could use to prepare for their GCSEs. There were advertisements for businesses, reviews of concerts, small ads for jobs and simple articles about youth-orientated matters. All that was missing was some focused activities that would guide them through their reading, but how on earth was I to transport dozens of copies of this quite heavy magazine back to England?

Suddenly, the idea hit me that all I needed to do was

cut out the relevant items, stick them onto cards, add a few questions and tasks and dole them out. The only problem was that it would cost a fortune to photocopy them. At this point, I had the idea to copy a concept that already existed in schools: that of the "reading library". For a number of years I had been doing freelance work for a company called Mary Glasgow Publications. Their speciality was making colourful magazines for pupils to subscribe to and read at home. Commercially speaking, this was a brilliant idea, because it locked them into a subscription mode, something that has become far more prevalent in the internet age. The people who wrote and produced the magazines weren't teachers, so they needed contributors like me to write teachers' notes, containing suggestions for how to exploit the materials in the classroom. This was my job, a very tedious one, and massively time-consuming, because I was such a slow typist.

The ideas person at Mary Glasgow was obviously bursting with them, because they also came up with a concept for French classes called "*Bibliobus*" (the French word for a mobile library). This was a box of about thirty small books, mostly in comic strip form, for pupils to help themselves to and read. I used "*Bibliobus*" myself, and it was lovely to see an entire class of pupils with books in hands, each reading something different from their neighbour. It seemed so much more natural than everybody doing the same thing at the same time.

When the time came for Mary Glasgow to publish a German version, which they called "*Lesekiste*", they asked me to write some of the books. This turned out to be massive fun, as I had to teach myself the skills of writing comic strips, entailing doing detailed artwork briefs for the designer to work on. I took the opportunity, when writing these and subsequent similar books, to include a strong social element. Some of the themes I tackled included racism, bullying and cruelty to animals.

So, on the storm-tossed ferry, my concept popped into my mind fully formed: GCSE-style reading activities, to be carried out individually by pupils and presented in the form of a reading library. As "independent learning" was also a "buzz" educational concept at the time, it fitted in perfectly. I regret to say that the planned romantic weekend was slightly ruined by me spending the entire time dashing in and out of tourist offices, restaurants, food shops, swimming pools etc, and stealing their brochures and menus.

Returning to school, I was eager to try out the idea, and spent several evenings cutting out the relevant items, sticking them onto A4 cards, writing the accompanying tasks in longhand and laminating them on the school machine. This final step was essential, because I hoped for the cards to be used multiple times, and without being laminated, they would quickly disintegrate.

In subsequent weeks, I began to find teaching a lot easier, because, without exception, the pupils absolutely adored the concept, far more so than I could ever have anticipated or dreamt. From the most gifted to the least able, they all appreciated the freedom it gave them to work at their own pace, unpressurised and not in competition with anyone else. I kept a couple of sets of answer sheets on my desk and when each pupil had finished the tasks, they simply came up, borrowed an answer sheet and marked their work themselves. As they were writing the answers in their own exercise books, there was an immediate saving of time, effort and money on photocopying, which had become redundant. Above all, there was no marking for me, the teacher, to do.

Word soon spread in the staff room that there was a new resource around, so I made sets for all my colleagues and felt a warm glow when they reported the same reaction: enthusiastic uptake from the pupils and less work for them. After a few weeks, it was time for the termly meet-up of Hampshire language teachers, which took place in a teaching centre in Winchester. A feature of those get-togethers was a "show and tell" session, where people shared knowledge of new resources they had come across. When my turn came, I did a practical hands-on session, using the newly invented cards. That was when I realised that my brainwave had traction; the teachers were all over them, begging me to make sets for them, and then phoning me up, asking for multiple sets for their colleagues, their friends, other schools and, by the way, did they also exist in French and Spanish and were they also available at other levels?

My immediate thought was, if these local colleagues are so keen, maybe there might be a demand for them elsewhere too? I approached Mary Glasgow Publications, as I was already freelancing for them, and sent a copy to their commissioning editor. After a couple of weeks, I received an enthusiastic reply saying that they were, indeed, interested in publishing them. But there was a problem - or at least there was as far as I was concerned. They wanted to make changes. This, I was later to discover, was typical of the attitude of big publishers. Because they employ a staff of editors and developers, they can't resist fiddling with a concept. In particular, they are wary of things that seem simple. I knew, because I had been using them for such a long time, that there was no need to make any changes to the resource, and that the changes they were suggesting would actually make them less effective. When I look back on it now, I realise that Mary Glasgow did me a massive favour.

I owe a huge debt to my friend Paul Dominy. Paul, like me, was a manager of small-time rock bands and lived in Gosport. Outside of music, we would occasionally meet up socially. On this occasion, he had invited me to an Indian restaurant he had recently got to know in Portsmouth. He had made friends with the manager and there was some discount on offer so, always up for a bargain, we boarded the Gosport Ferry and headed over the water. I remember the exact place we were in as we were walking into Portsmouth and I was explaining to him my dilemma.

"Why don't you just do it yourself?" he asked.

"What do you mean?" I replied.

"Publish it yourself."

"I'm not a publisher."

"Well, you could be."

"No, I couldn't."

"Why not? What's preventing you from being a publisher?"

"I don't know how to do it."

"It can't be that difficult. What did you do when you couldn't get a record deal for your band?"

"We put out an indie single."

"Exactly. And how did you do it?"

"We just did it."

"I rest my case. Just do it."

I had finally seen the light and, back in Winchester, paid a visit to Sarsen Press, the small printing company I had used for making posters and flyers for the band. After rejecting a very expensive and unnecessary method called "encapsulation", which would have made the cards virtually indestructible, Tony Hill, the proprietor, quoted me a figure of £2,000 for an initial run of 100 sets of 30 laminated cards and bags to put them in. Also sitting in the office was a man who was to become not only a good friend, but also my designer for the next few years, David Eno. David volunteered to work on the design to make the product look less amateurish, and to prepare them for print.

Now it was time for a top-level conference in the Gray family. In the fifteen or so years since returning from Germany, we had managed to save a grand total of nothing, mainly because the salaries of a midwife and a Scale 2 teacher were so low, and mortgage interest rates so astronomically high. But still sitting in my bank account in Germany was the tax rebate I had received in 1976. This was a "rainy day" fund, our little nest egg, to be accessed in case of a major emergency. Did Paul's idea qualify as enough of an emergency to spend our life savings on? We had to decide.

In the end, the decision was easy. Birgit and I both agreed that we wouldn't be prepared to go into debt, as most start-up businesses do, but that it would be worth doing a trial run, and if we lost all the money, at least we wouldn't be much worse off than we had been previously, and we'd have learnt a lesson. I went back to Sarsen Press, took a deep breath and placed the order.

It was only then that we started to consider advertising and marketing. In my heart, I knew there would be a demand, but I had no idea about how to get the message out. This was a long time before you could rely on Facebook and Google to do that for you. How were we going to tell people about "Carte Blanche" (we had to give it its obvious title, after checking that no other resources of the same name existed)?

It was Birgit who came up with the idea that we initially used. We needed lists of the addresses of secondary schools, but how were we to obtain them? Simple, by telling a white lie. We rang local authorities around the UK, pretending to be parents who were going to be moving into their area, and needed to decide which secondary school to choose. Please could they send us a list of details? Then we went to Ryman's and bought thousands of A5 envelopes, which we addressed by hand to the Head of Languages at each of the schools, adding a second-class stamp to each. We then inserted the flyer that David had designed for us, complete with an order form at the bottom, and took the envelopes to the local post office. To add an air of professionalism, we decided it wouldn't look good to have a normal street address for the business, so we signed up for a PO Box, to which any responses could be delivered. The omens were good, because my lucky number is 7 and the number we were allocated was PO Box 71, Winchester.

The most crucial decision was what to call ourselves. Back

in band-managing days, the drummer Paul Bringloe, who was later in life to become a professional cryptic crossword compiler, had christened me Gary Revilo, as an anagram of my name. For lack of a more attractive choice, we decided to call ourselves "Revilo Language Cards", thus lumbering ourselves for a couple of decades with a proportion of people who would pronounce it as in the word "revile", which sounded pretty disgusting.

Then, all we could do was to sit back and wait. I decided to leave it for a week before checking, and went back to normal work. At that time, I was cycling to and from school, and my route took me past the main post office in Winchester, so I finally decided to take the plunge and pop in on a sunny late Monday afternoon. I actually knew the official on duty, a post office veteran called Stan, who sometimes did shifts in our local village PO. "Hang on a minute," Stan said. "I'll just go and check."

My heart was in my mouth, and I was convinced that he would come back empty-handed, but when he reappeared, he was carrying a bundle of envelopes so big that he could hardly hold them all. "Here you go," he said, "that'll keep you occupied for a while." I stuffed the envelopes into my rucksack and set off on my bike in the beautiful sunshine along the Itchen Navigation canal towards home. I stopped at a waterside bench and, with bated breath, started to open the envelopes. One of the things we had decided to do was offer a "free sample" service, with a box to tick if that was what was required. Some of the envelopes simply contained sample requests, but the majority were actually full-on orders.

Most exciting was that most of them also contained a cheque. It seemed that we were in business, and I was almost shaking with excitement.

Now it's time to cut a long story short. Before long, our house was transformed into a mini-factory, because the cards came in individual piles that had to be collated. For example, from each pile we had to take one number 1, one number 2, one number 3 etc, and eventually accumulate a full set of thirty. Card collating came to be known as "doing round and rounds", with all the family joining in.

From day one, there was administration involved, including record and book-keeping, further advertising, packing and posting etc, etc. There was one obvious candidate to be in charge of the finances and general organisation. Do you remember me mentioning how good at maths Birgit had been at school? I am not one for national stereotyping, but it was a blessing for us that she also had what is often seen as a German trait: good, clear, reliable organisational ability. In the years to come, this was to be a much-treasured advantage for us, because I was fine on writing the materials, but not very good at keeping an eye on day-to-day administration.

In the following years, Revilo grew into quite a successful little publishing company. We decided early on that we were going to keep it as a small partnership of just the two of us. Sometimes I speculate whether borrowing money and making the whole thing much bigger (which was not only possible but also very tempting) would have been a better option in terms of long-term sustainability. Birgit was happy in her work and not in the position to take on much more, and I was a writer but definitely not a business-minded person. I'm pretty sure we might have ended up richer but a lot less happy, if we had not agreed to keep it a small family business.

There was still plenty to do though. After "Carte Blanche", we succumbed to demand and produced German and Spanish versions, and after that, we made what we called "Junior" versions for lower down the school. Finally, we created advanced versions for sixth forms. After a few years, we were able to calculate that roughly 75 percent of all UK secondary schools were using one or other of our products.

One thing I had to make sure of from the start was that we weren't breaking any copyright rules. It would have been possible for me to write new content in the style of "realia", but the whole point about "authentic materials" was that they needed to be authentic. Before publication, I wrote to the originators of all the materials, to gain written permission to reproduce their printed matter for educational use. As the vast majority of the material was for publicity purposes anyway, the responses were almost always delighted, showering us with piles of similar items. Some of them asked for small payments, which was fine. Only a couple refused permission altogether, so we replaced them.

Back in those non-digital days, the latest craze for listening to music was the Sony Walkman, or "personal stereo". I began to notice that almost all pupils had one of these devices, which led me to a second, perhaps more decisive brainwave. Why not harvest the potential of the personal stereo for offering the listening practice that was so vital in preparing for the GCSE exam? The same principle applied as for the reading cards.

Currently, the only way to offer listening practice was for me to stand at the front of the class operating a tape recorder, and for everybody in the class to listen at the same time to the same item. As with the reading, this was not helpful to the less able, who might need to listen several times to the same audio before understanding it, while their more able colleagues might get it on first listen.

The idea of giving them the freedom to work individually at their own pace seemed irresistible, and the personal stereo offered this option. While on an exchange visit in Hamburg, I noticed that a department store was offering cheap imitation Walkmen at a knock-down price. I phoned Bill Hubert who, bless him, agreed to free up some funds from the school to purchase a class set of these plastic personal stereos. I was so lucky to have such an open-minded and trusting head teacher.

Before I could get this new concept into full swing, I had to create the relevant audio materials. I wrote scripts for twenty-five 5-minute pieces of French audio and enlisted the services of an audio engineer, with whom I had worked on music projects. He was also in a position to mass-produce cassettes, which were, in fact, the cutting edge of audio technology at the time. Using some French people I knew in the area who had bilingual children, we then recorded the first set of "Eurolab", a box of 25 short cassettes, all different, just like the reading cards.

Exactly the same technique applied: students helped themselves to the cassettes and the accompanying question cards, listened as often as needed, using the fast forward and rewind buttons on their Walkmen, and then fetched an answer card and corrected their own work. As all this was done on headphones, it made for a blissfully quiet ambience in the classroom. Once again, Bill Hubert made a point of bringing school visitors into my room when such a diligent activity was taking place, as an example of modern-day teaching methods.

Putting together a box of "Eurolab" (it was a miracle nobody else had already copyrighted that name) involved even more frantic collating sessions. Each tape had to go into an individual case, then all 25 tapes had to be secured and encased in bubble wrap, before being inserted into a large cardboard box and a label attached to it. Also in the box were the question cards, which needed to be collated, plus the answer cards and a transcript for the teacher. Products like this, which were so work-intensive, would never have worked for a big publisher, as there was so much effort and so little profit involved. But we had found our unique little niche and were happy in it.

Marketing had become a lot easier, since we discovered that there were, in fact, companies that would mail out advertising material on your behalf. No more scribbling on envelopes for us. The only problem for me was that the Revilo work was expanding so much that it was hard to keep up with the day-to-day teaching activities. This led, over a period of years, to a gradual reduction of my hours at school – first, a three-quarter timetable, then a half, finally dwindling to nothing. I likened it to gradually coming off drugs. Being cautious by nature, I was reluctant to give up all my reliable salary until I was confident that we could live on the income from the business.

Revilo lasted over twenty years in all, during which time we published scores of items. All the reading cards and boxes of audio tapes were eventually produced at different levels and in various languages. We added grammar practice cards and also some popular little things called "Eurosigns", which were designed for labelling schools in foreign languages. The idea of this was to create an inclusive European-style atmosphere in a school building, back in the glorious times when European wasn't a dirty word. Eurosigns were ridiculously complicated to sell, because each order contained a different combination of labels. The only space we had to collate them was on our double bed.

We also created something called "Last-Minuters", which were tiny packs of revision cards, designed for people to use in the last few weeks leading up to their exams. Because these were supposed to be bought by individuals, we devised a method whereby teachers could order on behalf of their pupils, and we ended up sending out thousands of boxes full of multiple sets of "Last-Minuters". This was extremely labour-intensive, but by now I was free to organise my own life and the whole thing was non-stop fun.

Part of the marketing of these resources entailed attendance at various conferences and exhibitions round the country. The most notable of these was the annual "Language World", which took place at a different university each spring. Here, we would set up a stand and promote our products to passing teachers who were attending the conference. We were always the smallest stand, usually dwarfed by huge edifices created on behalf of the major publishers, but our little stall permanently had a crowd of people gathering around, because word about the "autonomous learning" aspect was out. Evidence of "pupil autonomy" was something that school inspectors were looking out for, and teachers were increasingly desperate for materials that would help them with this.

Birgit turned out to be a complete "natural" as a salesperson, something that ran in her family, because her father had been in sales of auto parts. She also had the required toughness and determination to make sure that nobody walked away without placing an order, while I mainly stood around feeling a bit embarrassed, because boasting about my own materials seemed very naff.

Something then happened which made me pretty resentful. In the main, we were looked upon with mild amusement by the big publishers and pretty much ignored, although not even they could have failed to notice the interest we were generating. The 1990s and early 2000s were a heyday for educational publishers in the languages field, because not only were languages compulsory to GCSE level, there was also plenty of government funding around. Teachers, for example, who wanted to buy some Eurolab boxes but didn't have enough money in the departmental funds, could make a bid for finance from the local authority. We always felt that it was unlikely that the big publishers would copy us, because the levels of profit were not high enough.

On top of that, we had an enormous Achilles Heel. The essence of educational publishing is instant obsolescence. The idea of a course book is to make it as disposable as possible, so that after a couple of years, it falls to bits and needs to be replaced. Our big selling point, by contrast, was that you only needed to purchase each item once and it would last forever. Although this was fantastic for marketing, it also meant that our entire business model was fatally flawed, because once the pack had been purchased, it never needed to be bought again.

One day, a friend of ours, who had another small publishing company, was on a train heading for a Language World exhibition in Manchester. In the same compartment was the head of the language resources department of a major publisher. Our friend overheard him shamelessly telling a colleague how good Revilo resources were, and how they had decided to go into competition with us by producing something similar. Sure enough, within months, they had come up with a pack that, I suppose, could have been looked upon as a compliment, such a blatant imitation was it.

On closer examination, I realised that, just like Mary Glasgow before them, they had been unable to resist making it more complicated and introducing too much in the way of fiddly, unclear activities. With ours, you simply couldn't go wrong. My mantra to teachers was, "All you need to do is plonk them on the table, say 'help yourself' and sit back and watch". This was manna to overworked and exhausted teachers, and our strapline of "No photocopying - No preparation - No marking" was exactly what they wanted to hear. The proof of the pudding was in the eating, as they discovered that there really was nothing else for them to do, and that the resources worked entirely on their own. The imitation resource put out by the big publisher was a flop, and was soon abandoned. I never forgot that publishing director, though, as he was to haunt my life in an equally unpleasant way later on.

Not all our publications were successful. An attempt to enter the potentially lucrative EFL market took a lot of effort and ended in failure. I created a large pack of English reading cards and we attended a number of EFL exhibitions in places like London, Brighton, Paris and Berlin, but they never took off. I hadn't realised that one or two publishing conglomerates had a stranglehold on the entire worldwide EFL market, and that the teachers could be very conservative in their attitudes. In Germany, as I should have realised, teaching techniques hadn't really progressed, and the idea of pupil autonomy hadn't caught on at all. Teachers still liked their pupils to sit in rows and be lectured, and the thought of them wandering around the class, helping themselves to learning resources, was complete anathema to them.

When I eventually produced an English version of "Eurolab", it failed dismally to sell, because no teacher would have allowed Walkmen to be used in class. What's more, some of them criticised the contents and language on the tapes, which I had made sure was colloquial and up-to-date. Considering that it had been written and recorded in modern-day England, I was quite offended by their arrogance and accepted that the EFL market would never be for us.

We also didn't succeed in getting into the primary school market. In the early 2000s, government policy switched to encouraging the teaching of a modern language in primary schools, but it wasn't supported by sufficient finance or expertise. Existing primary teachers, most of whom had no knowledge of a foreign language, were expected to teach something they knew little about, on top of an already crowded timetable. I thought that a set of primary level reading activities would help them to solve that problem, but I went against one of my golden rules: simplicity. Because it was necessary to add a vocabulary guide and a pronunciation tape to the package, it was more complicated to use. Although "Carte Blanche Primaire" received some praise, sales were mediocre. It didn't turn into the bonanza I had hoped for, largely because times had changed and the levels of funding in schools had plummeted.

It was time to embrace technology. Luckily, my designer David Eno was a tech-whizz and was able to set me up with templates, with which I could create huge amounts of interactive activities, both for listening and reading practice. The templates were perfect, because I didn't need to have any technical knowledge, but still could do all the data inputting myself. We had recording sessions in Germany and France, and I found two great illustrators to create the visuals. One was the boyfriend of a French "*assistante*" in Winchester, who was a talented artist with plenty of time on his hands. The other was the now retired Head of Art from Henry Beaufort School. He was very gifted, and his style was unusual enough to put a distinctive mark on our interactive resources.

All of them came out initially on CD-ROM, because the internet wasn't yet prominent, and certainly not in schools. At last we had the chance of making a decent profit, because manufacturing CDs in large numbers could be done at low individual cost, and sold at a high mark-up. Most of them were sold into schools with a so-called "site licence", which allowed any of their pupils to access them as often as they wanted, if they were put onto a school network. These items sold very well throughout the UK, because they were so economical for tight school budgets. An attempt to sell them individually to pupils, as we had done with the "Last-Minuters" was less successful, because it was putting an administrative burden on the teachers, who had to order on behalf of their students. Already, it was becoming clear that levels of motivation and commitment among language teaching staff were beginning to decline.

The signs that the success of Revilo would be limited were already in place. On top of the aforementioned Achilles Heel, there was another rule of diminishing returns taking place, with school budgets being slashed. We had saturated the market and, while other publishers sent high-pressure sales teams into schools, we had no such option. The final nail in our coffin came when "languages for all" was abolished in the year 2010. This meant that our main market (lower ability pupils who were being forced to do a GCSE language and needed to be motivated) was gone. Language resources in schools were no longer in anything like the demand they had been in a few years before. With our focus on German, we were particularly vulnerable, as German tended to be the first language to be dropped.

We had one more roll of the dice, however, and I am still quite proud that we were one of the first publishers to offer online resources. David Eno adapted our existing digital materials to be accessible online and we set up a subscription model, which we thought would be very attractive. I fear we might have been slightly ahead of our time because, when talking to teachers about it, we noticed a clear intimidation and reluctance to embrace this new approach. Now it's commonplace, but then it wasn't, and we had neither the clout, the money nor the marketing skills to make it work at a market-leading level.

Chapter 6

ROCK 'N' ROLL FAILURE

(i.) A matter of course

R unning parallel to our little business was my work for other publishers. Initially, these projects, for the likes of Mary Glasgow, Longman and Hodder, were small-time resources shared with another author, so the income would tend to be tiny. The ultimate ambition, to which I admit I aspired in my pipe dreams, was to write an actual course book. Because these sell in large numbers and are heavily promoted by the publishers, there was a small number of writers, especially in the heyday of "languages for all", who made themselves extremely wealthy. The most prominent of these was a famous creator of French course books called Rosi McNab. She had worked for various publishers, but now was pretty much the author of choice for Heinemann, the biggest languages publisher in the UK. Rosi was quite a star. She would waft the round the exhibitions on the lookout for ideas, and you could see all the delegates looking at her in awe. The rumour was - and I have no reason to disbelieve it - that she had made so much money from writing for Heinemann that she had been able to purchase herself a castle in Scotland, where she had a garret for writing. As Rosi had the golden touch, she was always the one who was commissioned to write the next course.

There always would be a "next course", because of the strange structure of British education. Every couple of years, there would be a change to the syllabus and the GCSE specifications. Sometimes, these changes were relatively minor, but the publishers would always use them as an excuse to launch a new course. They convinced teachers that they needed to entirely replace the previous course, which they had sometimes only invested in a few years before. There was massive rivalry between the big publishing houses, because if you could persuade a school to invest in Part One of a five-part course, you could assume that they would be buying materials from you for years to come.

Another aspect of the clear built-in obsolescence was the concept of workbooks. These were normally cheaply-produced black and white items, with activities designed for pupils to write their answers straight onto the pages. From a marketing point of view, this was genius, because each year, a stock of workbooks would have to be purchased for each new cohort. Anybody writing workbooks could be expected, if they were on a royalty, to earn an income from them for years to come. As I was quite experienced in writing such activities, I aspired to write some workbooks, but how did you go about obtaining such work?

Once again, it was the kindness of a good friend that did the trick for me. In contrast to the majority of employees of big publishers, who tended to look down their noses at small fry like us, I got to know the senior languages consultant at Heinemann, Trevor Stevens. Trevor was a small person, invariably dressed in what I thought was a shockingly tasteless green suit, and quite out of my league, status-wise. But one day, he turned up at our stand and we got into conversation. After about half an hour, we had already reached slapping-each-other-on-the-back-and-declaring-each-other-to-be-best-friends status, as we quickly discovered we had a huge amount in common. We were both German specialists, who had worked in the country and had great affection for it. We also shared a warped sense of humour and a healthy degree of cynicism about the world of educational publishing.

It wasn't long before Trevor had given me the right contacts to ask me to write some workbooks for Key Stage 3. These were for their current German course, which was called "Logo". In a way, I suppose it might have been a test of my ability and reliability, and presumably I passed that test, because not long afterwards, I was offered my dream job, to write a full GCSE German course book at two levels.

I may have rose-tinted spectacles in hindsight, but I can recall no downside at all to the writing of "Logo" GCSE level. I was allocated a freelance editor, with whom I hit it off, both personally and professionally. She had a way of conveying criticism in a manner that didn't offend, as she would write lengthy suggestions for improvements in pencil all over my manuscript. Truth to tell, most of her ideas were a lot better than mine, and we ended up with a good quality product, which was popular in schools for near-on a decade. Over the years, Heinemann sold tens of thousands of these books but, as German was a minority subject, the numbers were dwarfed by potential sales of the French equivalent. Would I ever reach that Holy Grail? Only time would tell.

The "built-in obsolescence" concept meant that one course would follow another, and also that all the publishers would be putting together competing courses at any one time, so my reputation as a speedy compiler of workbooks meant that I always had work. Living in a small house with young children was a slight hindrance to the deep concentration and vicious deadlines that had to be adhered to, so I would sometimes disappear for a week to some remote place where there were no distractions. I wrote "Logo 4" in a tiny apartment in Sitges in Spain, where the blinds got stuck in the "down" position, so I didn't even have the option of looking out of the window. Numerous workbooks were written in freezing, tumbledown caravans in Bridport, Swanage and Dorchester. One French project was completed when I went and did some dog-sitting for a rock musician in his mansion in France. Unfortunately, I managed to lose his beloved dog on the slopes of Mont Ventoux, but thankfully it reappeared in the nick of time, after two days of panic.

Wouldn't it have been nice to end these reflections with a success story? In the year 2000, I wrote a book about my parallel career in rock music. The theme was that, despite my enthusiastic efforts, everything I did was doomed to end in failure. My music journalism was only in small-time papers, not the big magazines. My band management didn't end in any hits, and my promoting career, while enjoyable, was financially debilitating. The previous chapter might have given the impression that I had ended up as a successful educational writer, but the truth is rather more depressing. Among the occasional triumphs, there were far too many disasters and let-downs.

Nothing was smooth in the world of Revilo. Because of the nature of our resources, it was only economical to build up large stocks, which we kept in our garage, in the hope of selling them long-term. Unfortunately, the stop-start nature of the curriculum meant that, on certain occasions, our stock became obsolete overnight. One particularly clear example of this was the day in the mid-nineties when the powers-that-be suddenly decided to switch the questioning at GCSE level from English questions to "target language tasks". Here's a very simple example of what that meant: Whereas previously a question might have said, "What animal is being referred to?", to which the answer would have been "a cat", now the task would instead say, "C'est quel animal? A: un chien B: un chat C: une souris."

This innovation was brought in more or less overnight, so, at a stroke, our vast stock of cards became unsellable, because they no longer fitted the national criteria. We had to take van-loads of redundant laminated cards to the dump and throw them in a skip. Even that wasn't straightforward, because the laminating procedure meant that they weren't recyclable, so we had to be quite surreptitious while disposing of them. The other side of the coin was that I now had to sit down and create, from scratch, entire new products in French, German and Spanish, or face oblivion. In one respect, this was quite good, because the hapless teachers were forced to buy new sets to replace the ones that were no longer usable. On the other hand, it was a big financial challenge, and we were lucky that sales were indeed healthy, and we were able to recoup the investment.

Surely lightning couldn't strike twice? Indeed it could, because another horror was on its way. In the year 1999, the Euro was introduced. All our resources were liberally spattered with references to Marks, Francs and Pesetas, so once again, these were now unusable. Not only did we have to replace about a third of all our stock, we also had to rush around making new recordings for the cassettes. Whereas in the "target language" debacle we had merely had to create new question cards for the listening resources, this time we had to record new versions of about a third of the audio. This double whammy was nearly a killer blow for us, as, once again, we had to throw away mountains of items that would have been perfectly adequate, had it not been for this sudden change of policy.

Arguably, the nadir of my doomed attempts at achieving a best-seller came courtesy of my old friends Diesterweg, in Frankfurt. Because "Sag Mal" had sold quite well in the UK, I suggested to them that an English version might work. Doris Jacoby had long since retired, and there was a team of enthusiastic young editors in place. They even agreed to put some money into the project, and sent one of the editors over from Germany to supervise the recording sessions, which took place in an expensive studio in Notting Hill. I went along to sit in on the recordings and, to my amazement and disbelief, found that, among the actors they had hired, were Timothy Bentinck and Carole Boyd, respectively David Archer and Lynda Snell in "The Archers". I was completely star-struck and breathless, scarcely able to say a word to them during the sessions. The two of them and the other actors were sniggering at the stilted language I had created, not really appreciating that it had to be compatible with certain grammatical concepts. They were right, it was terrible, but I still feel a warm glow at the thought of being sneered at by Lynda Snell. Needless to say, we had completely misjudged the German market. Sales were pathetic and the whole project was viewed by all with embarrassment.

All was also not well on the course book front. My hopes of becoming the new Rosi McNab were not to be fulfilled, because she still had plenty of energy and continued to write course after course. But the quality of "Logo" had not gone unnoticed by other publishers, and I was approached by Nelson Thornes, a new company that had been created by the merging of two educational publishers. They summoned me and a co-writer to their headquarters in Cheltenham. We came away full of excitement, as they commissioned us to write their new GCSE French course, using the same editor who had helped me with "Logo". This was a joyous project, from which we all gained a huge amount of pleasure. The publishing director was a very businesslike man, who revelled in casually referring to projections of the huge amounts of money we would be likely to make. Luckily, he did come good on giving us a decent advance on which to live, as we both gave up all other work for six months, in order to get it written in time.

I still don't really understand what happened, because we and the publishers were both delighted with the end result, but within the company, something was happening. The executive who had commissioned the work disappeared, and Nelson Thorne set up some kind of collaboration deal with one of the examination boards, who deemed the books not suitable for what they had in mind. Instead, they said, they were going to commission an entirely new course, to be written, as was increasingly to become the style, by a committee of six different writers. Our newly-completed course, which went by the uninspired name of "Voilà", was duly withdrawn and pulped, before more than a tiny number of sales could happen. To this day, I still receive royalty statements from the publisher, showing virtually no inroads being made into the advance.

To show good faith in us, I and my co-author were taken on as part of the team writing the new course, but it was a truly horrible experience for everyone involved. We had a different editor, who was very hands-on and deeply critical of more or less anything we submitted. There was a terrible feeling of tension, unhappiness and thinly disguised hatred throughout the creation of this resource, which nonetheless did eventually sell a good number of copies.

Battling with editors is something that occasionally crops up in publishing. They often seem to feel obliged to justify their position by insisting on changes that are not only unnecessary, but often make the activity worse than it was before. The problem is caused by the fact that the editors' background is in publishing rather than teaching, so they aren't in a position to understand what activities work in the classroom and what don't. Often completely mesmerised by the specifications of the exam boards, which themselves are run almost entirely by crusty old retired teachers who've lost the plot, certain editors demand that you include activities which you know damn well are never going to work in class. Any teacher will tell you who is likely to survive in a rowdy classroom and who will sink without trace. Among good candidates for teaching oblivion are not only inexperienced young editors, fresh out of university, but also politicians who pontificate about education. As we teachers always point out: "That person wouldn't last five minutes in a classroom" - and it's bloody true.

Back at Heinemann in Oxford, I was approached by an executive from their international division with a very exciting prospect. Their idea was to adapt all our existing Revilo resources into plastic-wrapped packs for sale all over the world. All they needed to do was license them from us and modify them, which seemed an excellent prospect to me. When the executive took me out to lunch, she was mentioning eye-watering potential amounts of income, to the extent that when I went home and told Birgit, we were dancing round the room with joy. Unfortunately, when we left the restaurant, the executive found that she had got a parking ticket and was so furious that she stormed off in a rage, not even saying goodbye, despite my total innocence in the matter. In the event, two items were actually published, but the executive had long since been replaced, a new policy had come in and they didn't even bother to market them. The advance I received was considerably smaller than what she had promised, and sales were so negligible that I never even received a royalty statement.

My big moment finally seemed to have come when my dear friend Trevor informed me that Rosi McNab was retiring. Heinemann, which had now been taken over by the international conglomerate Pearson, was working on a new French course (as we know, they were always working on a new French course). I had proved my worth with the success of "Logo", and they would like to ask me to write their new GCSE French course. Yippee! The Holy Grail that I had been seeking for so long was finally within my grasp. There was just the small formality of writing a sample chapter and submitting it for approval, which I did in about a week.

Around that time, I had made a bit of a fool of myself by buying what I thought was a bargain vehicle, a very strange Korean contraption called a Perodua Kenari. This was the first time I had ever bought a new car, but it was so cheap that it wasn't much different to finding something second-hand. Sure enough, the moment it was out of warranty, it broke down, so I took it to a garage in Chandler's Ford, near Winchester. After a couple of days, the mechanic rang me to tell me that it would be impossible to get the parts to repair it, and that the only option was to scrap it. That was how I found myself heading, on foot, towards Chandler's Ford, a distance of about four miles, in order to pick up the hopeless vehicle and take it to be scrapped.

I was in quite a bad mood, which wasn't helped by a very sad encounter with my ex-Head Bill Hubert, who lived locally.

Bill had retired and, during the chat we had after I bumped into him, I realised there was something wrong, and that it was clear that the first stages of dementia had started. I was reflecting sadly on this when my phone rang. On the other end was Trevor, who said that he had something to tell me, that he had to tell me in person, and was at that very moment driving down the M3 towards my house. I explained where I was and suggested that he should come and pick me up, to give me a lift to the garage.

When Trevor arrived, his news was not good. They had recently taken on a consultant, who used to work for another publisher. This consultant had been given the task of reviewing my sample chapter and had reported back that it was not of the required quality. His advice was that they should not proceed with me, but instead engage a different author. This consultant was the very same person who had been overheard on the train to Manchester, all those years before, in the process of stealing my autonomous learning idea. I gulped at Trevor's news, but quickly accepted that, if that was the case, there was little I could do about it. As an afterthought, I asked Trevor who would be commissioned to do the work and the answer was a bit of a shock: it was none other than the consultant himself.

The consultant and I would often bump into each other at exhibitions from then on, but not many cordial words were exchanged. He went on to write a number of other courses for Pearson and become very successful indeed. He was the new Rosi McNab, whereas I was fighting over the remains of a rapidly dwindling business. Revilo was on its last legs. Low school funding, constant changes in curriculum demands and the gradual devaluation of languages in secondary schools, plus of course our famous and fatal Achilles Heel, meant that the business was no longer sustainable. The final straw came when I was summoned by our bank manager and informed that they were no longer willing to extend our overdraft.

(ii.) Adult material

A year or so before Revilo came to an end, I made a terrible mistake by plunging back into the world of face-to-face teaching. Particularly humiliating was the fact that it was motivated by pure greed. Someone I knew at the local university told me I could get £40 an hour for teaching German to adults in the evening. That seemed a huge amount of money for me, and I was confident that the work would be easy, so I signed up with alacrity. I should have remembered, from my days of teaching adults back in Bremen, that it is very different from teaching children. You can't just tell them to be quiet and get on with their work, and you can't stop them from being inattentive and making irritating comments. Above all, because they are paying for it, they can be as critical as they like about your techniques.

The whole experience was absolutely awful, far from the doddle I had anticipated. The book they gave me to teach from was so monumentally unsuitable that it had to be ditched and I had to write all the resources myself. I had to spend hour upon hour preparing enough material for each

90-minute session. The woman who was running the evening classes was drunk when she attempted to describe the admin I was required to undertake. Serve me bloody right for being greedy in the first place.

Despite the fact that they had loosely been divided into groups by ability, there were vast differences in level within my class of about twenty students, so it was impossible to pitch any general teaching at a class level. If you managed to hit the right standard for a third of the class, it would leave another third sulking because they couldn't keep up, and a final third looking bored because the material was beneath their dignity. Worst of all was the fact that only a proportion of the students would turn up to any given lesson, so trying to plan any progression into the course was pointless, because so many of them would have missed a previous session. The motivation of the various participants could vary from those wanting a little bit of language to use on their holidays, to some who wanted to undertake quite serious study.

There were also huge differences in age, approach and character. I rapidly learned to hate their communal guts, and boy, was the feeling mutual. The final straw came when I was assessed by a lecturer who spoke not a word of German, yet still saw fit to justify his existence by criticising my teaching. I won't swear to it, but I'm pretty sure I told him to stuff his job up his arse.

(iii.) End of the road

One thing I badly wanted was for the name and the legacy of Revilo not to disappear completely. As we had been declining, another small UK languages publisher had been making a rapid rise. Called Linguascope, it was run by a very dynamic and inventive young Frenchman, and had caught the imagination of teachers, in much the same way as we had twenty years before. Without much hope, I wrote to him and asked whether he would be interested in buying Revilo, because I'd noticed that, in previous months, he had snapped up a couple of other small publishers. It was hard to see what he could do with our materials, but I think part of his strategy was to clear rivals out of the way, because he immediately showed interest. He wanted to take our cards and adapt them into the fashionable form of downloadable resources, where overheads were vastly less onerous than ours. But, more than that, he definitely had his eye on our digital online subscription items. This was an area in which Linguascope specialised, but they didn't have any exam-specific materials like ours. The assumption was that, with their marketing skills and clout, they would pretty much be able to take on our online offering and market it straight away.

I had a thrilling meeting in their trendy, bustling Shoreditch headquarters, during which I was made an offer of enough money to make a relatively comfortable retirement a possibility. All that was required was for a contract to be drawn up, which was done by Linguascope's solicitor, and due to be signed a week later. In preparation for this, David Eno, who had created the online platform, travelled to London to demonstrate the system to Linguasope's bunch of techies. David reported back that the session had been cordial and optimistic, so I signed the contract and sent it to be London to be countersigned.

It was a couple of days later that I got an email from Linguascope. After extensive examination of our materials, they had determined that the software used to create them was incompatible with their system, so incompatible, in fact, that no amount of adaptation would make them workable. They were therefore withdrawing from the deal, with immediate effect.

I had allowed myself to get over-excited, because everything had seemed so positive, so the come-down was pretty unbearable. We tried to find a way to limp on, but in the end we had no option but to close our baby down. Rather than just let it disappear completely, I again contacted Linguascope and offered them the entire business, including our banks of artwork and scores of resources, for a small fraction of what they had originally offered. They accepted this and adapted a couple of items, before moving on with their own programme.

The dream of a comfortable retirement, far less a castle in Scotland, was never achieved but now, in my seventies (don't tell anyone), I am nearly as busy as before, still plugging away, writing workbooks and revision guides for several of the bigger publishers. In fact, excuse me, I'd better get on.

(iv.) After-school activity

The other day, on a nostalgic memory trip, I drove past the Steiner school where I spent my first year of education. It seemed entirely unchanged, and as far as I know, the Waldorf principles have hardly moved with the times. They acknowledge the existence of computers and technology and make children aware of their dangers, but they are not used in day-to-day teaching. Institutions like this have benefited from the government's policy of encouraging "free schools".

During the same journey, I paid a visit to my old private secondary school, described in Chapter 1. It wasn't term time, but I was interested to observe that virtually nothing had changed physically in half a century, apart from the fact that everything seemed much smaller than I remembered it. Delightfully, Ye Olde Fishe Shoppe was still going, although it, too, was closed, so I don't know whether they still play "Sing Something Simple". The most surprising change at the school was some brash, tasteless branding in the form of huge logos on hoardings surrounding the sports pitches.

Looking at the primary school department, I wondered how it had changed in the interim. I'm sure the modern-day equivalent of Miss Lowry wouldn't have many of the freedoms that she had then to teach in her own way, because despite their independence, even private schools are closely monitored and inspected. I know quite a lot about government-imposed restrictions, because my daughter has taught for ten years in London primary schools, where people are constantly looking over your shoulder to make sure that you are teaching precisely what the authorities have decided you must teach. Highly restrictive specifications about content and a huge excess of largely unnecessary testing mean that children's education is now dominated by those "grey men in grey suits" who have been mentioned so often in these pages. Yes, the very ones who got out of teaching because they couldn't teach.

A few years previously, Richard Shephard arranged for the two of us to pay a proper visit to the school. The Head seemed a pleasant enough chap, and it was nice to see girls around the place. As with most other cathedral schools, there are now female choristers, an innovation for which Richard himself is largely responsible, because he was the first to introduce this piece of equality when working as choirmaster at Salisbury Cathedral School. Nonetheless, the sense of elitism still left me cold, especially when it became apparent during the conversation that they were hoping we might contribute to the school funds - very amusing - and after the meeting, we were left in the hands of the chief fundraiser. I actually know a guy who currently teaches in that school. His background was in highly eccentric and left-field rock bands. I know he's a good teacher, but he does have a gigantic beard, like so many of the staff had in my day, so maybe not everything has changed.

Richard Shephard himself became an internationally famous classical composer, as well as spending a lifetime in private education and being a very big luminary in the high society of York. Oddly, we remained good pals, and in January 2020, Birgit and I visited him, as we had done so many times before. He had been gripped by motor neurone disease and was a shadow of his former self. Most distressingly, his sense of humour had declined. It was a matter of great sadness to me that I wasn't even informed of his death and found out about it by chance.

All those farm labourers that I worked with as a student died young. The work was grindingly hard, involving breathing in diesel fumes all day, as well as dust from the corn and chemicals from the fields. In just a few decades, their skills have had to change dramatically, because the machinery has grown bigger and bigger and more and more computer-controlled, requiring entirely different abilities.

UEA has grown into one of the leading teaching and research institutions in the UK. Switch on any programme on Radio 4, and the resident expert will almost always be Professor So-and-so of The University of East Anglia. Student life could hardly be more different from those carefree Sixties days. With the vast fees and loans now required, students make sure they get their money's worth by working hard and fast for their qualifications. There is no longer a campus music scene and, post-Brexit, international exchanges and partnership schemes are complicated and few and far between.

The German school system has been able to resist the temptation to constantly change and innovate. Oddly, considering the country's reputation for industrial success, the education system has been very slow to embrace IT, and lessons are still largely based on full-class teaching, with blackboards and chalk having been replaced by whiteboards and sharpies. There have been minor changes, but in general, the school system remains pretty much as it was when I worked there in the Seventies. The *"Abitur"* is now based on a points system, but testing methods are still much the same as back then, with the essay-style tests now called *"Klausuren"* rather than *"Klassenarbeiten"*. Teachers remain well-paid, highly-respected, largely autonomous and with total job security. Interestingly, although Germany has some of the highest educational standards in the Western world, children start school there a full two years later than they do in the UK. It's interesting to speculate on how the UK manages to waste 24 months of a child's life, but it probably has something to do with the endless testing and the kind of nonsensical time-wasting bureaucracy that has been mentioned so often in this book.

Wolf Lingstädt, who was such an influence in my early teaching, died at a very young age from a rare form of cancer, which struck him in his forties, leaving a wife and two small children. The genial Herr Mumme, the Headmaster at Waller Ring, passed away not long after retiring, but I am still in close touch with many of my colleagues from those days, all living very comfortable post-professional lives on their large pensions. Dear Dr Brinkmann faithfully sent me a Bremen calendar every Christmas, until, one year, they suddenly ceased. It wasn't that he had died, but I was later to find out that he had been gripped by a particularly severe form of dementia, which meant that his latter years were a great struggle for his family.

The Gymnasium Waller Ring celebrated its hundredth anniversary in 2014, and some ugly modern extensions have been added to its original forbidding building. It remains a beacon of solid education in a deprived part of town and is now noted for its achievements as a bilingual school, with much of the curriculum being taught in English. Latin, French and Spanish are now offered too, in stark contrast to its UK equivalents.

Henry Beaufort School in Winchester remains a more than adequate comprehensive, one of three roughly equivalent secondary schools in the city. By all accounts, though, the atmosphere now is completely different, and the signs were there even before I left. Bill Hubert retired and everybody assumed that Roy Bone would be a shoo-in to succeed him. He had, after all, done absolutely everything to deserve that, but Bill's job went to an outsider, who arrived determined to make his mark.

We teachers all knew the writing was on the wall from the very first staff meeting under the new Head, during which he lectured us about what he perceived as our complacency. We were all working in a school that had a lovely atmosphere, very high standards and superb results, and I, even after all those years, was still in the mindset of German schools, where the general attitude is, "Don't fix what doesn't need fixing". Within weeks, the tinkering started, changing the names of the tutor groups and the teaching blocks, altering the timetable and the shape of the school day, down to the menus in the canteen. Yes, the new guy was fulfilling his need to make a mark, before moving on.

The mark was achieved with rapidly declining standards and an atmosphere among the staff that changed from friendly interaction to bitter resentment. Angry resignations abounded, as people's lives became filled with uncertainty.

In subsequent years, successive Conservative governments began imposing more and more prescriptive demands upon teaching approaches and content, and self-respect among staff fell to new lows. The decline of languages was accelerated and the stability that had existed within our languages department gradually crumbled. A few years after I left, German was largely erased from the curriculum altogether. In an over-dramatic way, I laughingly compared myself to how the coal miners must have felt under Thatcher: You devote your life to something that is subsequently declared to have had no value.

I can hear myself being accused of hypocrisy here. On the one hand, I spent a chapter pouring derision on those teachers who ruined my secondary education by being allowed to teach whatever they wanted, largely unmonitored and without checks and balances. Yet, on the other hand, I am patting myself on the back for the teaching I did both in Germany and in England, with similar freedoms. One thing is for sure: In the current UK educational world, I would never be able to shut myself in the Club Room and teach through songs, games and fun, using my own themes and grammar topics. Surely I can't have it both ways?

Well, as it happened, I was being discreetly observed by a bunch of supreme professionals, who were judging me and my colleagues on our results, and the results were nearly always good. In almost all cases, the pupils were happy and achieving their full potential, being offered a wide variety of styles, techniques and relationships. If any of our methods had turned out to be unsuccessful, we would have been advised, in a polite and friendly way, to modify them. There was no attempt to fix things that didn't need fixing, and certainly no imposition from above of content that was impractical or pointless. So, as with most things in life, there is a middle way. Currently, we have swung wildly away from the centre and into an almost dystopian, Soviet-style world of mind control.

Upsettingly, Roy Bone never got to enjoy the sailing he had planned for his retirement, after faithfully carrying on as Deputy Head under the new regime. He contracted a rare and virulent form of leukaemia and died in 1998, far too young, a mere year into his retirement. Bill Hubert passed away in 2016, after a long and difficult struggle with dementia, and the funeral had to be relayed into the churchyard through loudspeakers, so large were the crowds of mourners. If you Google them, neither can be found – a shockingly sad reflection on the value placed on service to education.

Almost every night, I dream about teaching, and most of the dreams are very uncomfortable. In them, I am in a classroom, trying to achieve something that is unachievable. I am being asked to explain things that I don't understand. I try to communicate matters that make no sense, even to me, and I see in front of me a sea of baffled and disappointed children's faces. Teaching wasn't at all like that in real life; in fact, it was immensely rewarding. But every day, I give thanks that I was able to quit at the right time. I never turned into that farty old git of an out-of-touch pedagogue, you know, the one with the tweed jacket and the leather elbow patches. But it was a close thing.

Also by Oliver Gray

VOLUME
A cautionary tale of rock and roll obsession

V.A.C.A.T.I.O.N.
Cautionary tales of travelling without style

ALAB (with Eddie Hardin)
35 years of musical mayhem on the road with the
Spencer Davis Group

ACCESS ONE STEP
The official history of the Joiner's Arms

ZANDER
An Americana whodunnit

BANJO ON MY KNEE
A musical journey through the American south

POLLY IN MY POCKET
Cautionary tales of camper van life

All published by Sarsen Press, Winchester, UK
For more information please head to www.olivergray.com